JUN 6 '93

COLORADO MOUNTAIN COLLEGE   SP
JN5501967.M4   Menhennet, David.
                     Parliament in

1 03 0000040914

JN
550
1967-b-
M4

DISCARDED

D0955914

PARLIAMENT IN
PERSPECTIVE

Parliament in Perspective

A BACKGROUND BOOK

David Menhennet
and
John Palmer

DUFOUR EDITIONS, INC.

CHESTER SPRINGS

PENNSYLVANIA

For Audrey and Helen

© David Menhennet and John Palmer 1967
Library of Congress Catalog Card number: 67–73291
Manufactured in Great Britain
First published in the U.S.A. 1967
by Dufour Editions, Inc.
Chester Springs,
Pennsylvania 19425

CONTENTS

5

October the 11th. The army now turned out the Parliament. So we had no government in the nation, and all was in confusion. There was no magistrate owned or pretended, except the soldiers, and they were not agreed. God Almighty have mercy on, and settle us.

John Evelyn's *Diary* for 1659

Parliamentary democracy is not something which can be created in a country by some magic wand.

Jawaharlal Nehru, in a speech in Lok Sabha,
New Delhi, March 28, 1957

AUTHORS' INTRODUCTION

THE AIM of this book is to present a factual and balanced account of the contemporary role of the British Parliament, based on our knowledge, as members of the House of Commons Library staff, of its day-to-day activities.

We have taken a middle course between the extremes of criticism and complacency. Some criticisms of Parliament are polemical and alarmist; but there also exists in certain quarters a smug assumption that the British Parliament is perfect and that other countries have only to emulate it and all their troubles will be solved. The unprejudiced reader, we believe, will find that the truth lies between these extremes.

The British people are politically sophisticated and their parliamentary system, which has become an outstanding means for the effective government of a free country, is highly developed, complex and delicately balanced. The greatest danger inherent in such a combination is not that the whole system will be overthrown by a military coup or by a popular uprising, but that Parliament will be taken for granted, neglected and misunderstood. It may be true that Parliament to-day is under strain. But so it was in the seventeenth, eighteenth and nineteenth centuries, when it surmounted crises and strengthened its position within the constitution by adapting itself to meet the challenge of changing circumstances. It will surely meet the problems posed by the technical, social and other revolutions of the later twentieth century, but it needs positive public understanding as well as passive public consent if it is to continue to function effectively.

The book starts with two chapters on the nature of parliamentary government generally and on the historical development of the British legislature. There follows a central section which describes the actual workings of the House of Commons and House of Lords as part of a system of democratic government. The concluding chapters consider, *inter alia*, the world influence of the British parliamentary idea, and in particular the prospects for parliamentary systems in certain developing countries. In the course of the book we discuss achievements, difficulties and strains, but we hope that we have put them 'in perspective'.

A study as short as this cannot be comprehensive. The details of parliamentary procedure have barely been touched upon, and the specialist will be quick to realise the extent to which we have had to compress our account. However, a few suggestions for further reading are appended to most of the chapters. A much fuller list will be found in *Government and Parliament in Britain: a Bibliography* by John Palmer, The Hansard Society, 2nd edition, 1964.

For the book's inception we are indebted to Mr Strathearn Gordon, OBE, Librarian of the House of Commons. Our colleague Geoffrey Lock has saved us from a number of infelicities by kindly reading the typescript, and we also want to thank other colleagues in the Commons' Library for their helpful suggestions.

David Menhennet
John Palmer

August 1966

I
The Idea of Parliament

THE FUNDAMENTAL principle behind modern Parliaments is simple, but often overlooked or misinterpreted. Stripped of all incidental adornments, the *idea* of Parliament is that a balance can be struck between Authority and Freedom which enables both elements to come together in a fruitful working partnership. So close is the partnership that it is proper to speak of the fusion of those two elements in Parliament.

The problem of the interrelation of Authority and Freedom—whether in its metaphysical, moral, social or political context—has featured prominently in Western philosophy from the very beginning. To discuss that problem fully would involve little less than the history of civilisation: but we are primarily concerned, in considering the nature of parliamentary institutions, with the particular issue of political organisation.

Politics are to be found in those states or communities which admit to being an aggregate of many different members, interests and traditions; political activity arises where there is disagreement between individuals or groups as to how the corporate body of state should act, but where there exists at the same time a desire to arrive at a national solution to those differences. A solution adopted and enforced in the general interest of the state is an act of government, and as such it is not unlike the visible tip of an iceberg. Beneath the surface are hidden vast areas of political activity and argument, and it is the relationship between the summit and the infinitely bigger base of the iceberg which determines the political organisation of the state itself. A genuinely democratic community, equally removed from the extremes of dictatorship and anarchy, aims at tempering government (or Authority) with

Freedom, and vice versa. And the working relationship between the two has been embodied by many nation-states in the institution of Parliament.

The idea of Parliament is thus a political concept. But Parliament itself is an eminently practical, *institutional* answer to the problem of Authority and Freedom. Neither Locke nor Mill, for instance, would have conceded that Parliament provided the complete political solution, for it does not answer such basic questions as the nature of the state or the propriety of the rule of law. Parliament is an agreed constitutional means of bringing about that all-important fusion referred to above in the context of everyday national political life—no more and no less. Or, to express it differently, Members of Parliament are practising politicians, not political philosophers.

As the freely elected representatives of the people, Members evidently form the basis of the element of Freedom in Parliament. But the coming together, in some sort of national assembly, of chosen men and women to discuss their differences does not of itself provide the balancing element of Authority or government which any democratic community needs if it is to survive, and which is in any case an integral part of the idea of Parliament. In order that a free and representative assembly should become a Parliament, it is necessary that the Government itself should be a part of it. How this came about in Britain forms an important section of the following chapter. The immediate point is that any true parliamentary system is concerned with government as much as it is with the liberties of the subject, and that it is at its best when the working relationship between those two elements is smooth, balanced and effective. If Parliament were simply an isolated forum for the expression of public opinion (and there is a tendency amongst certain political theorists to restrict its contemporary significance in this way), then its role in the process of democratic government would be severely curtailed.

To take an extreme instance: an astute aspiring dictator might decide to further his own non-democratic policies by paying lip-service to some sort of popular assembly. He would listen, or pretend to listen, to all that was discussed and agreed; but he would not feel bound in any way to deviate from his predetermined course of action. In such circumstances Parliament might indeed become a mere talking-shop, a hotchpotch of 'feverish and sterile fuss', in the words of Dr Salazar. But a true Parliament, though its name rightly implies that its members talk amongst themselves, is not an excuse for largely abortive discussion. A British Prime Minister, as chief executive officer of the land, does not simply *tell* his Parliament that he proposes to re-introduce corporal punishment for certain offences: if this is his chosen policy, then he must legislate in and through Parliament to that end. The Chancellor of the Exchequer may inform Parliament, in his Budget speech, that he proposes to introduce a corporation tax and a tax on certain forms of gambling: but he is also obliged to bring in a Finance Bill to that effect, and to submit his policies to the critical scrutiny of the House of Commons. Parliament may mean 'talk', but it is talk to a purpose: the chief argument in favour of Parliament to-day is that it obtains results by democratic methods.

To emphasise in this way that the modern Parliament is no mere talking-shop is not to disagree with those who praise its value as a vehicle for public debate. On the contrary, J. S. Mill's description of the British Parliament as a 'congress of opinions' still has much point to-day. Parliament provides potentially unparalleled opportunities for the airing of all sorts of views, and at the same time for educating public opinion; and as recently as July 1965 a Select Committee on Procedure stated in its Report that one of the main purposes of reform should be to enhance the efficiency of the British House of Commons as a debating chamber.

However, these 'expressive' and 'teaching' functions do not of themselves constitute the essential and distinctive feature of Parliament. The latter has long shared such functions with other assemblies, organisations and media—the Oxford Union, the Trades Union Congress, the national and provincial press and sound radio have all, in their very different ways, served both to reflect and to instruct public opinion. More recently, the advent of television has provided Parliament with its most powerful and serious rival to date in this sphere. Whilst sales of *Hansard* have declined, the viewing audiences for television discussions of great political, social and cultural issues have continued to increase. Neither should we forget that much-praised fledgling, the 'teach-in', which, ironically, arrived in Britain just as Parliament was preparing to celebrate its seven hundredth birthday. The Oxford and Edinburgh teach-ins, which discussed the burning questions of Vietnam and of Rhodesia respectively, made a great impact on public opinion. This kind of alternative publicity has been interpreted by some as an indication of parliamentary decline, and there is truth in the claim that, relatively speaking, Parliament to-day is less outstanding as a congress of opinions than it was in Mill's time. But it is because Britain has a genuine parliamentary system of government, which encourages the free discussion of differences of opinion, that all these alternative forums of debate are possible. Furthermore, the latter eventually contribute to a more sophisticated and informed electorate: if universal suffrage is to have any effective meaning, an educated majority of voters is essential. Above all, however, it is important to recall that the *idea* of Parliament embodies far more than this public debating function: no teach-in, no television marathon can or should supersede Parliament's basic constitutional role as an instrument of democratic government.

Parliament does not embrace the complete sphere of governmental activity. The vast and powerful Civil Service (or its equivalent administrative organisation abroad) is outside Parliament. And Parliament itself does not govern. But it is the meeting-place of government—whether personified in an individual or in a group of persons holding executive powers—and of represented democratic interests. The description of

Parliament as a meeting-place is deliberate, for it implies that the two concepts of government and democracy confront and influence each other there. On the one hand, the executive power of the land is wielded through, though not by, Parliament; on the other, Members of Parliament themselves are involved in the business of government in addition to holding their representative functions. It is this fusion of the 'governing' and the 'democratic' spheres of political activity, this interchange of what Aristotle described as ruling and being ruled, which gives Parliament its modern meaning and importance.

A brief semantic digression may be helpful at this point. Soon after its first known use in the old French epic *La Chanson de Roland*, the term 'Parliament' came to acquire a more specialised meaning than its original simple 'conversational' connotation. In its latinised or French forms of *parliamentum* and *parlement* it appears in several English sources, round about 1240, to describe important assemblies at which the king discussed and agreed affairs of state with his tenants-in-chief. Whether great issues of war and peace were debated at these assemblies, or whether more localised matters of royal administration and the exercise of judicial powers were considered, the concept of a meeting or confrontation between Authority as personified in the king and the wider (if not democratic) interests of the magnates, was already present in those early 'Parliaments'. Significantly, the description 'parleamentum de Rumened' was applied retrospectively in 1244 to that meeting of King John and his barons at which Magna Carta was signed. A hundred years were to elapse before 'Parliament' became the generally accepted title which it is to-day; but already in the later years of the thirteenth century its political connotation was clear. It denoted an important assembly, a meeting between the king and his great men to decide matters which concerned (in the words of Matthew Paris at the time) 'the whole state of the disordered realm'.

During the long history of parliamentary institutions a number of important, even essential attributes have grown up around the central idea. Not the least of these have been the establishment of a truly representative assembly on the one hand, and the more recent advent of strong political party organisations on the other. The growth and contemporary working of these attributes are considered in the following chapters of this book.

It is idle to suppose that the nature of parliamentary institutions constitutes a simple, straightforward subject. Apart from the fact that the British Parliament alone has a long, complicated history stretching back to Simon de Montfort (1265) and beyond, we shall see that individual Parliaments differ in many respects amongst themselves. So important are certain of these differences that there can be no lack of sympathy with a study of the structure and functioning of representative institutions in 41 countries, which declared: 'the very term "Parliament" has still to be defined, and its definition is by no means the least of the problems that political science has to face'.* And yet—there is much to be said for seeking a simple common denominator between these different individual Parliaments. The danger of not seeing the wood for the trees applies in the field of parliamentary studies as much as it does elsewhere, and too much attention to the inevitably complicated detail of the subject can lead to the unfortunate situation where the fundamental idea behind all Parliaments is forgotten or misinterpreted. Throughout the centuries men have been searching for the best way of combining the dignity and the rights of the individual member of society with the national requirements of law and order, and of steering an effective middle course between anarchy and dictatorship. 'To form a free government,' said Edmund Burke, 'that is, to temper together these opposite elements of liberty and restraint in one consistent work, re-

*Parliaments, first published for the Inter-Parliamentary Union by Cassell, 1962, p. 3. (In the 2nd edn, which considers 55 countries this statement is not repeated.)

quires much thought and deep reflection.' Parliament is one solution. It is not the only answer; neither is it necessarily the best. But the importance of grasping the idea behind it, of understanding what it sets out to do, cannot be overstated.

In various corners of the world individual Parliaments to-day face the difficult, sometimes discouraging task of adjusting themselves to the complicated, ambitious requirements of the late twentieth century. In each instance, the current interplay and advance of economic and social, political and scientific factors must be taken into account. At the same time, a considerable amount of discussion about the position of Parliament in public and political life has been taking place. In Britain alone, there have been more comment and criticism on this subject during the last decade than ever before. Positive criticism is better than negative goodwill, and the fact that the majority of these discussions and plans for reform stem from a friendly anxiety about the status and effectiveness of (in particular) the House of Commons is in itself reassuring. Inevitably, however, proposals for improving procedure, and even the wider investigations of specific constitutional problems, are more often than not involved, detailed, closely-argued. They tend to focus on particular aspects of the subject such as Parliament's relationship with the nationalised industries, the prospects for electoral reform, the desirability or otherwise of specialist committees of the House of Commons, methods of expediting the Finance Bill, the accountability of individual Ministers to the Commons, and so on. Anson is analysed and Dicey dissected. This work is valuable and necessary, but a consequence is that, to the man-in-the-street, the discussion appears to be an excessively complicated, even esoteric pursuit in which he has little part to play. This is regrettable, since there is no valid substitute for a widespread and reasoned acceptance of the basic *idea* of Parliament itself. The existence of the parliamentary habit or frame of mind amongst the people themselves is the best safeguard against both dictatorship and anarchy.

Parliaments are not indispensable, and the notion that authoritative government needs to be tempered with a measure of organised democratic criticism and support has never been universally attractive. 'A man who feels it his duty . . . to assume the leadership of his people is not responsible to the laws of parliamentary usage or to a particular democratic conception, but solely to the mission placed upon him. And anyone who interferes with this mission is an enemy of the people.' Adolf Hitler was addressing the Reichstag on February 20, 1938. Hitler and his 'Thousand Year Reich' are dead, but looking around the world to-day, one is compelled to agree with Professor J. D. B. Miller that the single-party or one-man, despotic or near-despotic situation becomes more prevalent 'with each lurch forward of the 20th century'.* The essence of such a situation is the absence of recognised alternatives to a single-minded authority, and it challenges the basic idea of Parliament. It sometimes happens that democratic institutions are overthrown by a sudden revolution. More often, a country's existing system is gradually diluted or perverted until it loses not only its effectiveness but its very *raison d'être*. When this happens the people at large, through their indifference to, and lack of understanding of, the very idea of Parliament are themselves in part to blame. Boredom with established truths, as Professor Bernard Crick has said,† is a great enemy of free men.

Perhaps the sort of dangers instanced above are too extreme to represent an immediate threat, at least as far as Britain and other long-established parliamentary régimes are concerned. The political and constitutional history of this country, it might be argued, has not been lacking in great upheavals and transformations, yet Parliament has persisted. This is true, but there are other dangers, less obvious and less dramatic, yet equally real.

Let us consider the British constitution. Unlike most

*The Nature of Politics, Pelican edn., 1965, p. 206.
†In Defence of Politics, Pelican edn., 1964, p. 15.

modern states, the United Kingdom has no written constitution, no single authoritative document setting out the laws of constitutional practice. One important result is that much of our present constitution depends upon tradition and convention. There is a tendency to preserve the forms of old customs and institutions long after their original meaning and purpose have changed or disappeared. This is not necessarily a bad characteristic; on the contrary, it has certain real and stabilising advantages of the sort which enable us, for example, to hold on to the prize of a constitutional hereditary monarchy. The Queen reigns but she does not rule. Yet this tendency to preserve the form of an ancient institution, to consider the symbol rather than the current reality, has intrinsic disadvantages as far as Parliament itself is concerned.

Two hundred years ago Sir William Blackstone spoke of the sovereign and uncontrollable authority of the British Parliament which enabled it to do anything not naturally impossible. Today Parliament's superiority over the Executive remains apparently intact: but the reality behind appearance is that the power of Parliament has been eroded in many different ways. Indeed its contemporary 'sovereign and uncontrollable authority' has the practical effect of placing enormous powers in the hands of the Government. If such a trend were permitted to develop unchecked, we might end up by maintaining the *form* of a democracy, and nothing more. Now is not the time to argue in detail the real or alleged dangers of such twentieth-century developments. But the discrepancy between Parliament's symbolic status and its real powers emphasises the need to be quite clear in one's mind as to why Parliament exists at all, and to grasp the basic principle, or idea, behind it.

The dangers of mistaking the outward form of parliamentary institutions for the real thing are illustrated in countries where democratic government has for long been discarded, but where some kind of 'Parliament' or popular assembly lingers on. (Hungary still has its magnificent, neo-Gothic Parliament Buildings fronting the River Danube at Budapest, and the *Statesman's Year Book* records—correctly—that supreme power is vested in the Hungarian 'Parliament'.) A more subtle peril, however, is contained in what might be termed the growth of the 'presidential' concept of government in countries outwardly claiming adherence to the parliamentary system. There are two great forms of modern representative democracy, the 'parliamentary' and the 'presidential'. The United States of America openly professes and practises the latter system. The Executive, consisting of the President and his administrators, is separated by constitutional law from the representative assembly, Congress. There is no direct confrontation of the two bodies in Congress, because neither the President nor his 'ministers' can be members of the Senate or the House of Representatives. The President, in consequence, is not dependent on Congressional support for his tenure of office. Recognising its separate existence, Congress has made its own arrangements to ensure that the necessary balance between executive authority on the one hand, and democratic scrutiny and control on the other, is properly maintained.

Generally speaking, no such arrangements exist in countries where the parliamentary system is practised, since the Government is in Parliament, and an integral part of it. But supposing that the 'presidential' concept, under which the Prime Minister acquired increased personal powers and acted independently of the elected assembly, were to take firm root in this country (Dr J. P. Mackintosh, M.P., and Mr. Richard Crossman, M.P., have suggested that Britain already has Prime Ministerial Government*): there would be no compensatory provisions to restore the balance between authority and democratic control because—outwardly if not in fact—Britain would still have its 'Parliament'. This formal survival could then obscure the need for a complete overhaul of the constitution.

* In *The British Cabinet* (1962) and in the Introduction to Bagehot's *English Constitution* (Fontana, 1963) respectively.

Historically, there is no justification for beginning in this manner with a statement of the *idea* of Parliament. The British in particular have always been primarily empirical in their political arrangements, and every schoolboy knows that the oldest of Parliaments evolved slowly and unsystematically without any preconceived overall notion of the theoretical implications involved. Practice preceded and shaped doctrine. Further, the theory of Parliament fails to explain what might be termed its working mechanics—its composition, its methods of doing business and its involvement with all those other institutions, corporations and organised interest-groups which are active and influential within the modern nation-state. And finally, a simple statement of what Parliament is—or should be—does not tell us how well (or otherwise) Parliament carries out its obligations. The reader may find some guide through the labyrinth of these historical and practical considerations in the rest of this book. For the most part, the British Parliament holds the centre of the stage: it is the oldest by far of all living national parliamentary institutions and as such it is probably this country's most important contribution to world civilisation.

But the *idea* behind all Parliaments is at once an introduction and a touchstone for what follows. Acceptance of that idea means that the first step towards an honest perspective of Parliament has been taken: and the importance of that step, in a world in which the principle of democratic government is on trial, is immense.

Further Reading

W. Bagehot: *The English Constitution*. With a long and stimulating Introduction by the Rt. Hon. R. H. S. Crossman, Fontana, 1963. (Bagehot's work was first published in 1867.)
S. Gordon: *Our Parliament*, 6th edn., Cassell for the Hansard Society, 1964.
Quintin Hogg, Rt. Hon.: *The Purpose of Parliament*, Blandford Press, 1946.

2
Past and Present

NOT VERY long ago, on a rainy June morning so typical of
the uncertainties of British summer weather, the Lords and
Commons met in Westminster Hall to present their respective
Addresses to the Queen on the occasion of 'the 700th Anniversary of Parliament'. It was in the strongest sense of the word
an historical occasion. Simon de Montfort, Earl of Leicester,
who summoned his now celebrated Parliament to meet in
London during the first three months of 1265, was not making
any conscious or planned contribution to the development of
parliamentary institutions. Very probably he wanted to enlist
as much popular support as he could for his own cause against
that of King Henry III. But his Parliament was nevertheless
the first assembly to which both knights of the shires and
representatives from the cities and boroughs were called. An
essential step forward had been taken. The closing ceremony
of that Parliament, moreover, had been held 'before all the
people in the Great Hall of Westminster', in a building first
erected between 1097 and 1099 and subsequently recon-
structed with its present magnificent hammer-beam roof at
the end of the fourteenth century. No more fitting place could
have been found for a great twentieth-century parliamentary
occasion which linked the past to the present and anticipated
the future with a cautious and pragmatic, yet firm, optimism.

There have been many detailed histories of the English
Parliament (we cannot really speak of its 'British' counterpart
of to-day until at least the parliamentary Union of England
and Scotland in 1707). The present chapter will not attempt
to add to the number of such histories. But if we are to
establish contact with the realities of our modern parliamentary system a brief glance into the past is unavoidable for

several reasons. Not the least of these is the very antiquity of Parliament. A national institution is not necessarily great and worthwhile because it has endured, and Parliament has a number of well-meaning but false friends who tolerate its continued existence simply because it is so old. Mr John Grigg, writing in the *Guardian* newspaper in June 1965, felt obliged to protest against the cult of antiquity for its own sake: 'In Britain the most tedious event of the year will be the 700th anniversary celebrations of Simon de Montfort's Parliament. These will encourage every M.P. to feel that he as an individual is 700 years old, with all the wisdom and maturity which such a long life might be expected to confer. . . .'

Admiration for the long-established, if it fails to penetrate beneath the surface, certainly has its dangers, and not the least of these are narcissism and unreasoning opposition to change on the part of those most intimately concerned. But it so happens that the history of Parliament is neither insignificant nor irrelevant to its modern purpose and meaning. Common sense insists, moreover, that a proud and practical people would have dispensed with the Parliament at Westminster long ago if its defects and anomalies had not been outweighed, in their minds, by its virtues and plain usefulness. The real importance of Parliament's being ancient lies, not in the outward signs of its long history (though the traditional ceremonies and trappings possess some intrinsic value), but in the hard fact that it has proved itself by the rough, unsentimental test of time. Has Parliament a future? The question has been posed several times in recent years, and answered in different ways. Fair-minded people, however, will not attempt to answer that question without reference to the formidable past of their Parliament.

Stanley Baldwin once said in the House of Commons*
that, although the historian was able to understand and explain constitutional practice as it existed at almost any given time in the past, a living writer would find it very difficult to provide a full and exact description of the constitution of his own

* H. C. Debates 261, 5th Series, February 8, 1932, c. 531.

day and age. Not only has that constitution, in the absence of a central authoritative written document, evolved slowly and unsystematically but it is still changing and adapting itself in different ways to the requirements and the temper of each particular age. We cannot therefore say, neatly and precisely, what the role of Parliament within the constitution *is*. A better approach is to indicate what, in the course of historical development, Parliament has *become*. Sir Ivor Jennings pointed out that precedents 'create conventions because they have reasons of a general nature which relate them to the existing political conditions and because they are generally recognised to be sensible adaptations of existing conventional rules to meet changed or changing political conditions'.*

In broad outline, the history of the British Parliament has proceeded by the imposition of new precedents—often not recognised as such at the time—on existing practices and conventions. This applies as much to the details of parliamentary procedure as it does to the great doctrines of constitutional practice; many of the former make little sense unless they are considered in the light of long-standing custom and precedent. The House of Commons has its own standing and sessional orders, but these are amply supplemented by conventions which grew up in the course of the transaction of business. Some date back to Tudor times and before; and these 'rules' are still being added to by decisions made by the Speaker while in the Chair. Of the older of such practices, that of barring the door of the Commons' Chamber in the face of Black Rod, the royal messenger sent from the Lords, is a good example. It dates from those troubled times when the Commons genuinely feared interruptions of this kind (particularly from royal representatives), and nowadays symbolizes their infrequently used right to bar all strangers from their proceedings.

But we are mainly concerned here to trace the emergence of a few simple, general principles as central features of our own parliamentary system, to show what Parliament has be-

* *Cabinet Government*, 3rd edn., 1961, p. 8.

come rather than attempt to fix it at some artificial point within the framework of the constitution.

Britain is a parliamentary democracy, and the people are represented in Parliament by a House of Commons composed of 630 Members elected for a maximum of five years. Parliament to-day is collectively made up of the Sovereign, the House of Lords and the House of Commons and it is the elected assembly which predominates within the legislature. But, in the early beginnings, the faithful Commons were not represented at all. The origins of Parliament stretch back to the custom of the Saxon kings of summoning their great and wise men to give them counsel and support. The king was not then strong enough to rule with absolute authority; he needed the assistance of the powerful men of the kingdom. The Saxon Witenagemot was certainly not an explicit confession of the need for a constitutional (or limited) monarchy as we now understand the term and there were to be many subsequent set-backs. But it was an early pointer to future developments of that kind.

The Norman kings were, in their turn, attended by the court of their feudal vassals, or tenants-in-chief: high church dignitaries, earls and barons generally selected by the monarch in the light of the task in hand. These conciliar assemblies assisted the Crown in the business of governing by offering advice on all sorts of matters, ranging from the making of war and peace to judicial and even local administration. At first they were composed entirely of magnates or great men. Magna Carta itself, though its subsequent constitutional significance was considerable, was in essence concerned to protect the rights of powerful feudal proprietors against the abuse of the king's prerogative. There is certainly some truth in the famous gibe of Sellar and Yeatman, in *1066 and All That*, that the Charter of 1215 was a Good Thing for everyone—except the Common People.

But it was already becoming apparent to thirteenth-century English rulers that the combined resources of their personal revenue and of the baronial grants-in-aid obtained through their Great Councils were insufficient to meet those extraordinary expenses incurred when some national emergency, such as a war, arose. And so they hit upon the expedient of summoning representatives of those communities, or 'Commons', which made up their kingdom, in order to win practical support for their taxation proposals. A document of 1254 preserved at the Public Record Office shows how, during the absence of Henry III in Gascony, 'two lawful and discreet knights' from each of the shires were summoned to the 'council at Westminster' to see how they might assist the king in his great need for extra financial aid. This express connection with the raising of money marked an important early step in the evolution, within the king's court, of a representative assembly: for the knights were summoned *in the name of one and all*.

Community representation in those early deliberative and consultative assemblies which met at Westminster—and to which the term 'parliaments' was already occasionally applied—was taken a further step forward by Simon de Montfort when he brought together for the first time knights and burgesses at a discussion of national and political importance. Thirty years later, in the so-called Model Parliament summoned by King Edward I, the great principle that 'that which concerns all should be approved by all' was clearly stated. The Commons had arrived as partners with the Crown and nobility in Parliament.

They were unequal partners, however, and at first the knights on the one hand and the burgesses on the other were not wholly united in their mutual interest. (An echo of this division persisted well into the nineteenth century in the superior social status associated with a 'county' as opposed to a 'borough' seat.) There was in fact no House of Commons. An early indication that they were drawing together within Parliament was the first formal appointment in 1377 of a 'Speaker' who reported to the king the results of the Commons' deliberations. By that date, knights and burgesses were in fact meeting as a single body, with their own Clerk, and whilst it was almost a hundred years later before they achieved the full institutional status and privileges of a separate House of Commons there is no doubt that the beginnings of our modern bicameral legislature may be traced back to the mid-fourteenth century. There were the Lords, attending in answer to individual summons; and there were the Commons, present as representatives of the shires and boroughs. This unification of itself enhanced the authority of the Commons who, incidentally, were not allowed to forget their distinctive representative function. 'They are the servants of those who send them', declared a satirist in 1399, 'and if they are false to the men of the shires who pay their wages, they are not worthy of their hire'.

It was the growing realisation of their power, as representatives, to grant or withhold supplies for the Crown (much later, for the Government) which really placed them in an influential position. Financial authority, the holding of those precious purse-strings, lies at the very centre of our parliamentary history. Other countries have set up their democracies on the basis of reasoned political and philosophical argument; the constitutional history of England has stemmed largely from the raising and expenditure of public money. Although the rulers of Tudor England tended to summon Parliament only when they needed extra money, sixteenth-century Members realised that their presence in Parliament to grant money and supplies was a heaven-sent opportunity to press certain claims, to ask for the redress of grievances before they consented to the king's demands. Charles I later tried to dispense with such parliamentary methods of obtaining money. He failed and paid a terrible price. James II's lack of historical sense and vision not only brought about his personal downfall; it also enabled Parliament to reinforce its growing authority in the handling of national finance and, as a result,

25

COLORADO MOUNTAIN COLLEGE--LRC--WEST

in the government of the land. The Bill of Rights of 1689 specifically laid down:

> That levying money for or to the use of the crown, by pretence of prerogative, without grant of parliament, for longer time, or in other manner than the same is or shall be granted, is illegal.

The same document also stipulated that 'for redress of all grievances' Parliaments ought to be held frequently, a provision which aimed at ensuring that Parliament's continuing control over finance was not eroded by any royal attempt to govern without the support of the assembled Commons. In the years which followed, Parliament's authority grew steadily; for there were frequent and very costly wars which made the financial independence of the king a practical impossibility. But although the Commons were already the more powerful of the two assemblies, the Lords' power of veto over measures proposed by the elected Chamber remained theoretically unlimited until the twentieth century. In 1911, however, the Parliament Act swept away the veto of the Lords in respect of money bills (bills dealing *only* with taxation, public money and related financial matters), and the present high constitutional principle, so well expressed in Erskine May, came into being:

> The Crown [that is, in modern parlance, the Government] demands money, the Commons grant it, and the Lords assent to the grant; but the Commons do not vote money unless it be required by the Crown; nor do they impose or augment taxes, unless such taxation be necessary for the public service, as declared by the Crown through its Constitutional advisers.*

Only the Government may recommend the expenditure of public money; but the Government is in, and must legislate through, Parliament.

Parliament to-day has full, exclusive rights of taxation; and the fact that money cannot be raised nor its expenditure sanctioned except by Act of Parliament is the people's surest

* Erskine May, *Law, Privileges, Proceedings and Usage of Parliament*, 17th edn., 1964, p. 705.

26

guarantee that public and even sometimes private grievances will be fairly and openly discussed. But in order to draw attention to such real or alleged wrongs, Members must be allowed full freedom of speech—they must be able to ventilate shortcomings within the sphere of government without fear of repercussions on themselves or their constituents. The individual citizen's right to speak his mind depends on the privileged freedom afforded to his representative in Parliament. That freedom was already being formulated in the fifteenth century. In practice, however, this privilege was far from being a safeguard against incurring disgrace and imprisonment; and in Tudor times, after the Speaker had made his customary request on behalf of a newly summoned House of Commons, the Lord Keeper's reply—while granting freedom from arrest and freedom of speech—often contained a warning against the abuse of those privileges.

Queen Elizabeth I expressly forbade Members to 'speak of all causes'; 'She sayeth', reported the Lord Keeper on her behalf, 'no king fit for state will suffer such absurdities'. The story of one man's brave struggles in the reign of Elizabeth I for privileged freedom of speech—that of Peter Wentworth, M.P.—is recounted in Dr Horace King's *Parliament and Freedom*.* The struggle continued unabated during Stuart times until in 1689 the Bill of Rights laid down that freedom of speech and debates or proceedings in Parliament 'ought not to be impeached or questioned in any court or place out of parliament'. The winning of this right to free speech, and of the accompanying privilege of freedom from civil arrest except on a criminal charge, took a long time to achieve; like so much of our parliamentary heritage, they are closely bound up with, and should be viewed in the context of, the historical development of the nation as a whole.

There is no better commentary on the slow emergence of an independent, powerful House of Commons within the

* Chapter IX. (The author became in 1965 Speaker of the House of Commons.)

legislature than the history of the most honourable and onerous of its offices, the Speakership. More often than not, Tudor
Speakers presided over the Commons' deliberations in the
capacity of royal servants: they were the King's, or the
Queen's, men. In 1642 William Lenthall first publicly pro-
fessed the Speaker's allegiance to the cause of parliamentary
freedom when he told King Charles I, on bended knees, that
he had neither eyes to see nor tongue to speak 'but as this
House is pleased to direct me, whose servant I am here'. But
many years were to elapse before the great modern standards
of political independence and impartiality—taken for granted
now—were to become fully established. Despite the personal
prestige and achievements of Arthur Onslow (Speaker from
1728 until 1761), it was not until Shaw-Lefevre (1839–1857)
severed all political ties both in the Chair and out of it that
the Speaker emerged as the custodian of Members' collective
and individual constitutional rights and privileges.

At the General Election of March 31, 1966, Dr Horace
King stood as 'The Speaker' seeking re-election, not as a party
candidate, and he was not opposed by any official party
candidate (although this latter practice is not invariable even
to-day). 'A Speaker's duty', said Captain Fitzroy on being
elected Speaker in June 1928, 'is to defend the rights, privileges, traditions and independence of this ancient Parliament.'
Centuries of hard, sometimes bitter struggles for the independence and supremacy of Parliament are bound up in those
words.

Sir John Fortescue, a fifteenth-century Chief Justice, wrote
a treatise *In Praise of the Laws of England* in which he con-
trasted the absolute monarchy in France with the limited monarchy of England. Extraordinary taxation in England, Sir John
pointed out, required parliamentary consent. Further, the king
might not make or change *laws* without the consent of Parliament. The sovereign authority of Parliament was indeed later
to find its principal expression in the making of statute laws.
The real long-term significance of Magna Carta was its de-

claration that the king was subject to the rule of law; nearly 500 years later, the Bill of Rights elaborated and confirmed this principle, and linked it to the powers of Parliament to make and repeal laws.

Long before 1689, Parliament had been a legislature, but the Commons were slow to emerge as effective participants in the law-making process. As early as 1327 they presented a corporate petition—'the first Commons public bill'*—but the knights and burgesses were simply asking the king to enact certain provisions and had no firm control over the ultimate fate of their petition. Gradually their growing importance in the realm of public finance enabled them to insist more and more that grievances should precede supply, thus making them legislators as distinct from petitioners. This important transformation did not take place simply or smoothly. Although legislation by Bill instead of by petition became customary round about 1460, on subsequent occasions the Commons surrendered to the king their hard-won initiative by permitting him to levy certain taxes without their prior legislative consent. At other times the king himself dispensed of this parliamentary process of raising the money he required.

Despite its complex, often surprising history, however, legislation became and remains a prime concern of Parliament and in particular of the House of Commons. Successive Acts of Union in 1707 and 1800 respectively extended Parliament's legislative authority to the whole of Great Britain and Ireland (since 1922, Northern Ireland only). It is true that the great majority of public Bills to-day originate with the Government, and not in Parliament: that is an inevitable result of the manner in which twentieth-century parliamentary government has developed. But Parliament remains the legislature; for the Government is in Parliament.

The Bill of Rights, that great landmark in our constitutional history, has been referred to often. But England in 1689 was

* K. R. Mackenzie, *The English Parliament*, Penguin rev. edn., 1963, p. 27.

not subject to parliamentary government in the modern sense. First, there were grave imperfections in the franchise and in electoral methods which prevented the House of Commons from becoming a truly representative body. Secondly, the Government was not yet in Parliament. Parliamentary government to-day means that the political heads of the Executive are members of the legislature and responsible to it. The Government of the day depends for the success of its law-making proposals and for its survival on the majority support of the House of Commons, and most of the Prime Minister's Cabinet colleagues are chosen from amongst elected MPs. By this process, as we have seen, the operations of government and of representative democracy are integrated.

As might be expected, this integration, this transfer of power from the monarch to an Executive, politically answerable to Parliament, came about gradually and followed no pre-determined pattern or programme. The emergence of the Cabinet system is in fact a prime example of the historical and practical—as opposed to theoretical and speculative—basis of British parliamentary government, and until comparatively recently its existence was not even recognised by statute. In briefest outline, the Cabinet developed from within the Privy Council, an ancient body of royal advisers dating back at least to the reign of Henry III. By the time of William and Mary, this ancient Council had grown too large to be an effective instrument, and an inner élite of influential persons, who came to be known as the Cabinet Council, were seen to be the real force at the monarch's side. But it remained an unofficial body. The House of Commons was at first very reluctant to have 'placemen' amongst its members, and the Act of Settlement of 1701 stipulated that no person holding an office or place of profit under the Crown could be a Member of Parliament. (Had this provision not been quickly repealed the modern Cabinet system might have been stifled at birth.) The king, at the same time, had no wish to delegate his powers to his ministers: William III was 'a real working, governing king', as Maitland has pointed out.*

But King George I could not speak fluent English and spent much of his time in Hanover. His interest in, and authority over, his Cabinet decreased, and although George III subsequently made stout efforts to win back executive power the process by which the determination of national policy—the government—passed from the Crown to a group of influential ministers in Parliament had begun and could not be halted. Within the Cabinet, in the absence of the king, a 'Prime Minister' emerged as *primus inter pares*: Sir Robert Walpole was the first minister to be given and to deserve that name, even if the term was originally intended to be derogatory.

Walpole was also, and equally significantly, a member of the Commons. The secret of his power was twofold—his influence with the king and his leadership within the House of Commons, which lasted from 1721 until 1742 when he sustained two successive parliamentary defeats. His Whig ministry also pointed the way towards that doctrine of party solidarity within the Cabinet which to-day forms an essential tie between the Prime Minister and his ministerial colleagues. This political unanimity of the Cabinet, moreover, binds the Government and Parliament even more closely together. Queen Anne might have been influenced by the Commons in choosing her ministers, but she did select them. To-day, the Prime Minister chooses his colleagues; he himself is a prominent party politician, and must therefore have colleagues who, with him, will be collectively responsible to Parliament, and in particular to the House of Commons. It is thus the composition of the latter which determines the political complexion of the Cabinet, and it is no less the majority support of Members which enables a Government to remain in office. The British system of government, because it is parliamentary,

* *The Constitutional History of England*, 1948 edn., p. 388.

31

is not despotic. Its authority depends on an elected House of Commons and, through the Commons, on the people themselves.

Party solidarity within the Cabinet, and the influence of strong party political organisation and discipline on Parliament itself, are further illustrations of the way in which important developments, largely unknown to the law and not officially recognised in Parliament, have imposed themselves on the traditional practices of an unwritten constitution and modified it to meet different political conditions. There has been, in the words of a contemporary Frenchman, Bertrand de Jouvenel,* 'a ceaseless fitting of ... basic principles to changing circumstances'.

History holds the key to a present understanding of Parliament; it tells us what the latter has *become* and warns us that it may develop and change in the future. This involvement in national history, moreover, helps to explain an outstanding feature of the British Parliament. It has always been an eminently practical institution, composed of practical men from different walks of life, and it has consistently pursued a practical purpose. Parliament has never been a seminar of distinguished political philosophers intent on perfecting a planned and logical parliamentary system. As Magna Carta stipulated over 750 years ago, 'no scutage or aid shall be imposed in Our kingdom unless by common counsel thereof. ... No free man shall be taken, imprisoned, disseised, outlawed, banished, or in any way destroyed ... except by the lawful judgment of his peers and by the law of the land.' The seeds of parliamentary government are apparent to us in these words: yet the barons who compelled an unwilling monarch to affix his seal to the Charter were acting selfishly and with a short-term practical purpose in mind. Much later the basic principle of 'grievances before supply' established itself as a cold, business-like instrument of parliamentary control.

* In *Government and Opposition*, Vol. 1, No. 1 (October 1965).

Parliament's past defeats the historian who would take us neatly from one constitutional document to another in a smooth continuous line of development. Similarly Parliament to-day, because it is bound up with the hurly-burly of national affairs, tends to perplex and irritate those who, while prizing its qualities, deplore its imperfections. Parliament may be imperfect, and if a modern Rousseau were to draw up a Social Contract for Britain to-day he might well plan a legislature very different from that which we have. But paper constitutions, many of them at least, have a habit of disappearing. Simon Bolivar, who dictated an unworkable constitution for Bolivia shortly before his death in 1830, bitterly reflected that treaties were scraps of paper, and constitutions, printed matter. The British Parliament is not entirely dependent on printed matter. Its practical character, though responsible for anomalies and anachronisms, also explains its astonishing long-term adaptability and resilience.

Parliament is therefore a legacy of practice. But it is also, in one important respect, a legacy of intent. The history of Parliament, simply stated as the rise to power within a bicameral legislature of an elected House of Commons, has reflected those democratic forces (sometimes inarticulate, often uncertain, but never completely suppressed) which since Magna Carta and before have made themselves felt within the framework of the state. The result has been neither anarchy nor communism, but the Queen in Parliament. The Commons' supremacy stands for the rights of John Citizen, of the average man: not to the exclusion of all class and privilege and not at the expense of strong central government, but certainly to the extent that individual self-respect and freedom have been preserved within the confines of established law and order. Because the history of Parliament is therefore the people's history, because its strength is that it reflects national character and aspirations, it is rooted in popular approbation and depends on the continuing understanding and support of the people. Only if the character of the British people changes radically will Parliament decline and disappear.

Further Reading

K. R. Mackenzie: *The English Parliament*, Penguin, 1963.

3
One Man, One Vote

BRITAIN TO-DAY is a democracy, but that word has been so much used and abused over the last 50 years or so that a brief consideration of its meaning is unavoidable. Almost every nation-state claims to be a democracy of sorts, and this proliferation of 'democracies'—from Britain to East Germany to Pakistan—has confused and diluted the significance of the concept. There is a temptation to abandon the term as worthless, its meaning stretched beyond all usefulness. And yet the false claims are made because the value of the idea itself is so universally recognised. It is still important, therefore, to distinguish between a true democracy and a system which, while borrowing the name, lacks some (or indeed, all) of the essential elements.

The original ideal, that all citizens should directly participate in all governmental decisions, is clearly possible of fulfilment only in very small communities, and even in them one would not expect pure democracy to be necessarily either desirable or, indeed, desired by everyone. While most people want to share in the political process and expect to be consulted, they do not themselves wish to be involved at all stages in the work of government.

Further, even in a comparatively simple type of community, specialisation and the emergence of experts would seem to be a condition of progress; and this corresponds to the tendency in human nature for a person to devote his best energies to his immediate task. The farmer will concentrate on his farming and the welfare of his family within a political system which he has helped to determine. He will recognise, too, that if good farming depends on expert farmers, the business of government in its executive aspects also demands experts. The ordinary man has a voice in choosing his representatives and through them influences the direction of public policy. But the detailed administration of this policy (whether by officials of the central government, by customs officers or by public health inspectors) calls for specialists in those fields just as the 'ordinary man' is a specialist in his.

If this is true even of comparatively small communities, it is clear that in a large, complex and densely populated country pure democracy, in the sense that it was supposed once to have existed in the Greek city-states, is out of the question. Not only is it impossible but, in so far as it can be imagined, it is likely to be inefficient, unstable, a hindrance to development and not genuinely desired by the majority of men. What then should democracy mean in a modern state? Lincoln's famous definition, 'Government of the people, by the people, for the people,' contains some of the essential elements. It follows from the size and complexity of modern society that government—in the sense of the formulation of national policy—cannot be carried out by all the people but will be undertaken by those who are *chosen* or elected by the people. But if choice in a democracy means election, a system of election does not necessarily ensure democracy. There can be elections without choice (as in Russia, where normally only one candidate is put forward) and there can be elections where the choice is imperfect because opposing candidates are denied equal freedom before the electorate (as in the last Portuguese Presidential election). There can be elections which are not 'by the people' because the electorate is deliberately limited or divided (as in South Africa), or because a section of the electorate is intimidated (as has happened in some Southern States of the USA).

Thus the process of election by itself is not a sufficient test of democracy: *all* the people must have a voice; the choice must be a *genuine* one between real alternatives which reflect differing views in the community; and the choice must be exercised in *freedom*: freedom both for the candidates and

36

the electors. These requirements amount to much more than 'government by consent of the governed', which is sometimes put forward as an adequate definition of democracy in the modern state. Hitler, at any rate at first, governed with the consent of the governed, and was, indeed, democratically elected.

This brings us to a further essential question to be asked of any country which claims to be a democracy: what is there to prevent the elected Government becoming a tyranny? What is there to ensure that it remains responsive to the will of the people? This most difficult question cannot be answered entirely in this chapter, and will come up again when we consider the Struggle for Power. Free elections are only part of the machinery of democracy: they are not ends in themselves.

Britain is a *parliamentary* democracy: that is to say, the choice which the people exercise is directed to the election of 630 Members of the House of Commons. This is not the only possible democratic system, but the whole development of British democracy both springs from and has contributed to the emergence of the House of Commons, the representative body within Parliament. Democracy by itself may have little practical political significance. The parliamentary system in Britain provides a focal point where the forces of democracy and government meet.

Democratic elements in the British constitution reach back into the distant past, but it is only in comparatively recent times that the constitution can be said to pass (perhaps imperfectly) all of the tests for democracy outlined above. The ideal of fully representative government ('of the people, by the people, for the people') did not exist in early times and was still quite foreign to such a writer as Bagehot in the mid-nineteenth century, but the principles of election (which can be traced in England back to the thirteenth century) and of representation are both deep-rooted in the country's history. (Although only parliamentary elections fall within the scope of this book, these are only the apex, as it were, of a much wider system of democratic election throughout the country. The direction of local government is in the hands of elected representatives on parish, rural or urban district, county or borough councils; and the election of officers and committees is a feature of the innumerable organisations which play an important part in local and national affairs—whether political parties, trades unions, professional bodies or learned or philanthropic societies.)

Even in the days when no one doubted that government was the *King*'s government, it was already established that the House of Commons, an elected assembly, existed to voice the grievances of the people at large and to propose remedies for them. The House of Commons grew to be the predominant partner in Parliament precisely because it was admitted that the Chamber which was elected by the people and which spoke for the people had the right to the decisive voice (in effect, the voting of taxes) in the government of the people.

At the same time, the House of Commons which won its battles for supremacy with the Crown was, judged by the standards of democracy, a very imperfect instrument. It is true that the Members were elected, but, before 1832 at least, the majority were returned for seats which were openly bought and sold, or seats which 'belonged' to certain well-recognised interests where the results were foregone conclusions. However, for all their careful management of the House of Commons, by a mixture of threats, cajolery, bribery and appeals to reason, the King's ministers could not prevent, under the pressure of events or mistaken policies, the drifting away of support. They also had to reckon with a minority of Members who prided themselves on their independence, and on the periodic recurrence of elections. Nevertheless, so long as many of the Members were elected by only a handful of voters, whilst bribery, corruption and intimidation openly flourished, then manipulation of the House of Commons by a small group (who might themselves be courtiers or peers and not elected at all) was open to those with sufficient skill and resources.

This obviously unsatisfactory state of affairs could not withstand the arguments of reformers—indeed some of the more blatant features of the system could hardly be defended by anyone except the Duke of Wellington. A further powerful factor in the movement for reform was provided by the growth of the industrial towns—entirely unrepresented in the Commons—and by the dramatic increases in population in the later years of the eighteenth century and the early years of the nineteenth. There was no sudden conversion of the ruling classes to the ideal of democracy as it is understood to-day, and reforms in the electoral system had to be fought for step by step. But by that process of gradualism so characteristic of the development of English institutions the reforms which at one time were fiercely contested, and which must have seemed to their early advocates impossible of fulfilment, have now all been accomplished.

The first Reform Act was passed in 1832. The Duke of Wellington said, 'The barriers of the constitution are broken down; the waters of destruction have burst the gate of the temple', but in retrospect it seems a mild enough piece of reform. Broadly speaking, the vote was restricted to the middle classes (and to men only, of course) by means of a property qualification, and the electorate only increased from about half a million to 720,000 out of a total adult population of 10 million. The Act also gave representation to the new and expanding industrial centres, and it swept away the 'rotten boroughs'. Nevertheless, the passage of the Bill gave rise to bitter parliamentary struggles, and its opponents only acquiesced in its passing after an election had clearly demonstrated the tremendous popular feeling for reform; Lord Melbourne warned the House of Lords that 'both the legislative and executive powers must yield to the popular voice or be annihilated'.

Reformers recognised the Act as no more than a small first step towards a democratic electoral system, and in 1838 the

'People's Charter' demanded universal manhood suffrage; voting by ballot; constituencies of approximately equal size; annual Parliaments; abolition of a property qualification for Members; and the payment of Members. Annual Parliaments (that is, a general election every year) were soon recognised to be impracticable for stable government, although the Parliament Act of 1911 reduced from seven years to five the maximum time allowed between general elections. Apart from this, all the reforms demanded by the Chartists—which seemed so dangerously revolutionary at the time and which apart from the principal 'Six Points' included the abolition of plural voting and the ending of the disqualification of paupers—have now been accomplished, but only over a long period and often against fierce opposition.

The franchise was extended in 1867 (the first major reform since 1832), again in 1884, and in 1918 universal manhood suffrage was achieved. The 1918 Act also gave the vote to women over the age of 30, and in 1928 women, like men, had the vote at the age of 21. Owners of business premises and university graduates were allowed two votes until 1948 when all plural voting was abolished and the position 'one man (or woman), one vote' was finally achieved.

Voting by secret ballot was introduced in 1872, and this first step towards the elimination of bribery, corruption and intimidation at elections was followed by the Corrupt and Illegal Practices Act, 1883, which had a dramatic effect. The average cost per vote polled at the election in 1880 was 18s. 9d. At the 1900 election it was down to 4s. 4d. and in the 1911 election fell again to 3s. 8d.*

It is impossible to achieve constituencies of exactly equal size without disregarding existing administrative and natural boundaries, but if one gives the word 'approximately' a fairly generous interpretation it is possible to say that we now have constituencies of approximately equal size, and boundaries

* C. O'Leary, *Elimination of Corrupt Practices at British Elections, 1868–1911.*

40

are regularly reviewed in order to take account of the growth or decline of population in different areas. The principal bias in the system is that Scotland and Wales have more seats per head of population than England.

The property qualification for Members was abolished in 1858, and the payment of Members was revived (for Members had received a sum for their expenses in medieval parliaments) in 1911, and is more fully discussed in a later chapter.

These are the principal landmarks, but a number of other provisions of the electoral law, although of lesser importance in comparison with such fundamentals as the franchise, are still essential for a fair and democratic system. Thus, *any* British citizen of full age who can find ten electors to sign his or her nomination paper can offer himself for election. (There are a few categories of persons disqualified from sitting in the Commons, such as peers, judges, lunatics and civil servants.) The only provision for dissuading large numbers of freak candidatures is that each candidate must pay a deposit of £150 which is forfeited if he receives less than one-eighth of the votes cast. Further, the amount which each candidate may spend on his election campaign is limited by law; the maximum varies with the number of electors in the constituency, but a typical figure would be round about £800. The intention is to prevent a candidate with large financial resources securing an unfair advantage by lavish expenditure on propaganda and other methods of persuasion. (Nonetheless, with general elections occurring on average every three years or so the expenses involved in mounting campaigns are substantial. In fact, most candidates rely largely on the local party to raise the money, and some receive contributions from sponsoring bodies such as trade unions.)

Every candidate may have an election address delivered free by the Post Office to every voter, and all candidates are at liberty to canvass, speak in public halls or on street corners, put up posters, send loudspeaker cars round the streets, and so on. The main parties are given time during the election campaign to put their case on television and radio. There are, of course, strict provisions to ensure that voters are free to record their choice, and that there is no possibility of tampering with the ballot papers or of falsifying the result.

In contrast to the controversy and struggles which attended the extension of the franchise, the law designed to ensure the fair conduct of elections has been enacted and revised from time to time largely with the agreement of all main parties. During this century it has been the custom, when the electoral law stood in need of revision, to appoint a conference of members of all parties, presided over by the Speaker, to advise on the amendments required. Such Speaker's Conferences have been appointed in 1916, 1929, 1944 and 1965. But although all the parties will agree on the fair conduct of elections, no party is likely to agree to any alteration of the *status quo* which it thinks may damage its electoral prospects. Also, the parties have been represented at the Conferences according to their strengths in the House of Commons at the time of appointment.

The first Conference, which reported in 1917, reached a great measure of agreement and most of its recommendations were enacted the following year. But the second Conference, which reported in 1930, achieved little because it was unable to reach agreement on proportional representation; and the third Conference of 1944 (which consisted of 17 Conservatives, nine Labour, two Liberals and four others), although it published many useful recommendations, reached a significant number of its decisions by majority vote and not unanimously. Only a few of the Conference's recommendations were enacted before the advent of the Labour Government in 1945 and it is hardly surprising that when the new Government eventually brought forward its Representation of the People Bill in 1948 it should have flatly reversed some of the decisions of the predominantly Conservative Conference—for instance, over the abolition of university seats and the abolition of plural voting. The Government was, however, able to deploy powerful arguments in favour of the steps it took, and the provisions of the 1948 Act have not been repealed by later Governments.

At the time of writing, another Speaker's Conference is deliberating on reform of the electoral system. Apart from such minor matters as the form of the ballot paper, the postal vote, the registration of electors, and so on, there seem to be only two subjects which might give rise to controversy. The Labour Party is in favour of reducing the voting age to 18, which is the qualifying age in all Communist and in some other countries. A much thornier problem, which divided the Conference set up in 1929, concerns the method of casting and counting votes. This issue is fundamental, but a discussion of it is best deferred until the workings of the present system have been examined.

Under the existing British electoral system the country is divided up into electoral districts (constituencies) of broadly equal electorates, each returning one Member of Parliament. Each elector has one vote, and the candidate receiving the highest number of votes is elected. The most graphic name given to the method is 'first-past-the-post'. The overall results of the system in the last General Election can be seen in the following table:

1966 Election	Total votes cast	MPs elected	Number of candidates	Share of total vote	Share of seats
Labour	13,057,941	363	621	47·9%	57·6%
Conservative	11,418,433	253	629	41·9%	40·2%
Liberal	2,327,533	12	311	8·6%	1·9%
Others	452,689	2	145	1·6%	0·3%
Totals:	27,256,596	630	1,706	100·0	100·0

Notes: The total electorate was 35,965,127. The 'others' included Communists (57 candidates), Scottish and Welsh Nationalists, Independents. The only 'others' elected were the Speaker and a Republican Labour candidate in Northern Ireland. Tables for earlier elections may be found in D. E. Butler and J. Freeman, *British Political Facts 1900–1960*, and B. R. Mitchell and K. Boehm, *British Parliamentary Election Results 1950–1964*.

43

So far as the electoral *system* is concerned, two things are immediately obvious from this table: one is the wide discrepancy between the percentage of votes received by a party over the country as a whole and the percentage of seats won; and the other is that it is the two main parties which gain from this discrepancy: 13 million votes gave Labour 363 seats, whereas 2·3 million votes won for the Liberals only 12 seats—the relation between the two parties in votes was 6:1, but in seats it was 30:1. This 'unfairness' is not a new or temporary feature of the electoral system,* and it is easy to see how it arises under the 'first-past-the-post' method of voting if one considers the result in a single constituency. The result at Uxbridge in the 1964 election was:

Curran, C. (Conservative)	20,519 votes	(43·6%)
Parker, T. J. (Labour)	19,866 „	(42·3%)
Goodall, R. (Liberal)	6,644 „	(14·1%)

The seat was won by a candidate who polled only a minority of the votes cast. In theory, similar results could be repeated all over the country and a party which polled less than 50 per cent of the votes cast in the country as a whole could win all the seats, leaving the other parties—one of which might poll 40 per cent or more of the total vote—with no seats at all!

The British method of casting and counting votes clearly leads to a result which is not exactly representative of public opinion and which therefore is not entirely 'democratic'. Why, it may be asked, is the 'first-past-the-post' system tolerated, when in such matters as the franchise and the fair conduct of elections a truly democratic system has been painstakingly evolved, and when methods of proportional representation have been developed and practised for years in other countries? The answer to these questions falls into two parts, one severely practical, and the other more theoretical.

* In the 1906 General Election, for example, the Liberals polled 49 per cent of the total vote and won 400 seats; the Conservatives polled 43·6 per cent of the total vote but won only 157 seats.

The practical point is that the two main parties are the beneficiaries of the inequalities of the system, though they too at times suffer from its vagaries, as in 1951 when the Conservatives won 26 more seats than Labour but received 0·8 per cent *less* of the total vote.* While supporters of minority parties may have cause for disgruntlement, the two major parties are unlikely to propose reform. Change in the electoral system in the past has depended either on agreement between the parties or on one of the main parties adopting for itself the banner of reform. The likelihood that a system which benefits *both* main parties will be changed is therefore small except in very special circumstances. Such circumstances arose in 1929 when the Labour Government depended for its existence on Liberal support. In return for this support it introduced in 1931 a Bill which, if enacted, would have led to the adoption of the alternative vote—a method which, though far from signifying complete proportional representation, would have given the Liberals a fairer percentage of seats in Parliament. The Bill passed through the Commons, was destructively amended in the Lords, and after the fall of the Labour Government in August 1931 was heard of no more. It is possible, of course, that the Liberal Party might once again find itself in a position to persuade one of the major parties to enact electoral reform in return for support in the House of Commons.

The more theoretical line of argument against electoral reform points out—quite rightly—that the adoption of either proportional representation or the alternative vote would be a real 'leap in the dark'; either system would produce results impossible to calculate. But what is reasonably certain is that a 'fairer' electoral system, by increasing the representation of small parties, would mean that an election which resulted in a clear majority for a single party over all the others would

* The Labour Party also received a smaller percentage of seats than of votes in the 1955 and 1959 elections. The Conservatives suffered in this way in 1945 and in 1966.

45

become the exception rather than the general rule. The deficiencies of the electoral system, it is argued, should be accepted because in normal times they do at least produce a decisive result. Elections are only a means to an end—their function is to create a Parliament and a Government, not to pursue the unattainable dream of pure democracy or numerically exact representation.

Further Reading

D. E. Butler: *The Electoral System in Britain since 1918*, 2nd edn., Oxford University Press, 1963.

J. F. S. Ross: *Elections and Electors*, Eyre and Spottiswoode, 1955.

4
The Struggle for Power

THE ESSENCE of parliamentary democracy is the recon-
cilement of strong, stable and efficient government and of
personal freedom: in particular, the freedom of the elector to
help choose and change those directing the nation's affairs. In
this chapter we are concerned mainly with the governing side
of the equation, with what is usually termed the struggle for
power, but which would, perhaps, better be called the struggle
for the right to govern.

This is no simple matter: it is an essential characteristic of
a parliamentary democracy that power is diffused, divided and
balanced between many different groups, whereas in a
dictatorship or an authoritarian régime power is concentrated.
Thus, we have to consider not only the supreme struggle for
government—the contest which decides the choice of the
administration to direct national policy—but also the balance
of power between the people and the Government, between
the political parties, between the House of Commons and the
Cabinet, and even within the Cabinet, between the Prime
Minister and his colleagues.

The struggle for the right to govern Britain (the outcome
of which is decided by the electorate at a General Election)
has been carried on for the last hundred years and more between two great political parties. For the whole of this period
there have only been two parties, at any given time, with the
clear possibility of obtaining a majority in the House of Commons, although for much of the period there have been smaller
—but often very influential—parties as well: Peelites, Irish
Nationalists, the Labour Party before the First World War and
the Liberal Party after it.

Criticism of the political parties—some of it perhaps well

deserved—is so common that their *necessity* in a modern parliamentary democracy tends to be forgotten. Complaints are heard that the parties are rigid and doctrinaire; that their policies are evolved undemocratically; that they engage in furious struggles over unimportant matters; and that they exercise, or attempt to exercise, dictatorial control over their followers. But however much truth there may be in these criticisms it is quite unrealistic to hold that the remedy lies in the abolition of parties. Nor can it be found in their proliferation; there is no reason to suppose that a number of small parties would suffer any the less from these faults. Professor Bassett, in his *Essentials of Parliamentary Democracy* (2nd edn., 1964, p. 32), provides an excellent summary of the case for parties:

> Party is essentially a unifying force. . . . No one can enter or belong to a political party without to some degree subordinating his own particular views or interests. Every political party involves the pooling of individual ideas, the adjustment of personal and sectional interests, and a measure of compromise in order to secure the maximum degree of common agreement . . . The notion that parties are uncalled-for intruders in a state of political harmony is, of course, fantastic. They do not divide 'the people'. . . . Without them, there would be a chaos of isolated individuals with conflicting interests and views.

Parties in their modern form owe their existence to the extension of the franchise since the middle of the nineteenth century. Whereas in 1860 the electorate numbered about 1,100,000 and in 1914 about 7,500,000, it now stands at nearly 36 million. A modern political party of any importance must be a mass party; as well as a national organisation it needs an efficient electoral machine in every constituency in the land and these will be very largely dependent on voluntary workers dedicated to returning their party to power because they believe that that is best for the nation. (Parties once did not bother to fight hopeless seats—at the 1900 General Election 163 Conservatives and 22 Liberals were returned unopposed—in agreement with the constitutional doctrine that what mattered in the formation of a Government was simply the number of seats in the House of Commons. It is now the practice for each major party to fight nearly all the seats, however hopeless, so as to gain the maximum possible total vote. A minor, but suggestive, acceptance of the democratic principle.)

No major party can hope to be successful if it represents only narrow interests, such as the Trades Unions or 'the City'. It may gain much strength from such groups and organisations, and there is no harm in that, but it must make a broad appeal to the nation as a whole if it is to have any prospect of success at the polls. The Labour and Conservative Parties both present themselves before the electorate as the party best fitted to be entrusted with the guidance of public policy in the interests of the whole community. Each has to thrash out, and present to the public in its manifesto, policies which will not only kindle the enthusiasm of its regular supporters but which will also attract the previously uncommitted.

The party leaders are themselves well aware of this necessity. The Conservative leader, Mr Heath, in criticising views put forward by the chairman of the Monday Club, Mr Paul Williams, a former Conservative M.P., has said: 'I thoroughly disagree with his views. I always have and I suspect I always will. They are not the views of the modern Tory Party nor of the great majority of people in this country. The Tory Party must always remember, and I . . . am determined it will remember, that it can never serve the nation by pandering to sectional interests. It has got to put forward policies which commend themselves to more than 13 million people. Otherwise it won't be elected to power.' (Reported in the *Observer*, January 16, 1966.)

The Conservative, Labour and Liberal Parties are in basic agreement on many issues: all the parties (with the exception of the British Communist Party and a few other small groups which attract insignificant popular support) accept the basic democratic and parliamentary framework of the constitution,* and they could all, without much exaggeration, be described as centre parties. The Labour party is on the political left, but it is not a revolutionary socialist party—the Liberals would often, it seems, be more ready to change existing institutions. The Conservative Party is a party of the right, but it accepts the necessity for change, and has often in its history been a reforming party.

It is commonly said that the aims of the parties are similar: all want to modernise Britain, all promise better housing, higher living standards, more roads, more schools. This does not, however, mean that there are not deep-rooted differences between the parties; it simply reflects the fact that the needs of the community as a whole are not impossible to ascertain and that many of the principal disagreements between the parties will arise not over those needs themselves but over the means of fulfilment to be pursued and the priorities to be employed. A rough consensus between the parties on aims (though not on means) is not a sign of political stagnation but a reflection of broad agreement in the electorate itself. The number of people who will support a party either of the extreme left or of the extreme right has been very small for a very long time.

Although the two main parties confront one another from opposite sides of the House of Commons, there is in fact no sharp dividing line between them. Rather, they shade into one another and together cover the political spectrum. Each major party is itself an amalgam of many different groups: each has its 'left wing', its 'right wing', its 'die-hard' and 'progressive' elements. The political differences between the extremes of the two parties (between, that is, left-wing Labour and right-wing Conservative) are very great. The

* However, Samuel Beer in his *Modern British Politics*, 1965, has an interesting chapter on the differing ideologies of what he calls Tory Democracy and Socialist Democracy.

gap between the extremes within either party may be considerable. But the distance between right-wing Labour and left-wing Conservative can be very small.

From this it may be argued, granted the necessity of parties, why have only two? Why do not the various groups within the big parties split off to form their own parties, each of which would be more coherent, more homogeneous, more clearly defined? There are a number of explanations. But the overriding reason is the knowledge that a splinter group or new party would stand, in the short term at least, virtually no chance of success at the polls. The overwhelming bias in the electoral system in favour of the two major established parties is well known both to practising politicians (who do not relish the prospect of sure electoral defeat) and to the electors, the great majority of whom prefer to vote for a party which has a chance of forming a Government. This consideration does more than anything to perpetuate the two major parties as coalitions of large numbers of people with only approximately similar views: splinter groups are formed *within* the parties rather than outside them.

Such groups are often ephemeral, but after one has died another is usually born. In recent years there have been several such groups within the Labour Party: 'Keep Left', the Victory for Socialism movement, and the supporters of nuclear disarmament* on the left wing, the Campaign for Democratic Socialism in the centre, and the 'Common Market group' on the right wing of the party. In the Conservative Party, the Bow Group exerts pressure on the left of the party while less overtly organised groups such as the Monday Club bring influence to bear from the right. Party policies as presented to the electors never satisfy the extremists, partly because they are compromises between the differing views within the party and, more important, because party leaders appreciate that

* Movements such as the Campaign for Nuclear Disarmament are not, of course, political parties themselves, but are designed to persuade the parties to adopt as their own a particular policy.

extreme policies will not appeal to the electorate. The more extreme supporters of either major party will be consistently disappointed on issues such as wholesale nationalisation or denationalisation.

This brings us back to the question posed at the end of the last chapter: if the nature of our electoral methods gives such a strong bias towards the two-party system should it not be reformed so as to give smaller parties a fairer chance?

There are many reasons why logic and 'fairness' in the electoral system should not be the overriding consideration. We have already touched on one reason for favouring the two-party system—namely, that each major party must then be a national party of broad appeal, wary of extremist policies and reconciling within itself narrow sectional interests. Further, the present system usually produces a decisive result, one party obtaining a clear majority of seats which enables it to settle down to a reasonable term of office in which to carry out its policies. It is quite certain that a more equitable electoral system would tend to promote minority Governments or coalitions. The minority Governments of 1924 and 1929 proved to be weak and unstable administrations; coalitions— except in time of war or national crisis—would be impracticable while the party system is in anything like its present form. The two peace-time coalitions of this century—the Lloyd George Government after the First World War, and the National Government of 1931—left a trail of bitterness and recrimination.

The Cabinet system and the way in which the House of Commons works also favour the existence of only two major parties: there are only two sides in the House and Members must vote 'Aye' or 'No' on every question, unless they decide to abstain. Efficient government requires a united Cabinet, and this will be more easily achieved if it is drawn from a single party. Above all, perhaps, our constitutional system requires a strong Opposition to criticise and scrutinise the Government's actions and to put forward alternative policies. Such an Opposition is only possible if the party in power is faced by a formidable and coherent adversary which can offer itself as an alternative Government. The knowledge, within each major party, that it may be called on to form a Government after a General Election, is sobering. It discourages wild criticism and acts as a strong curb on any temptation to make unreal promises to the electorate.

In human terms the two-party system also has strong merits. An outstanding politician wishes to grasp the reins of power in his own hands, and when two parties alternate as the Government he has a reasonable chance of doing so. There are deeper reasons too: it is not altogether fanciful to say that the two-party division corresponds to something in human nature:

> the real basis of division between the parties has been between those who stand, on the whole, for the maintenance of the existing ways of life, and those who stand, on the whole, for changes which are regarded by them as progressive. It is the old explanation, and it seems the only one that fits the facts. There are two main attitudes of mind, which may or may not be strengthened (they usually are) by considerations of economic interest. There are those who are, on the whole conservatively-minded, and those who are, on the whole, progressively-minded. This rather vague division . . . has its counterpart in the alignment into two great parties, the Party of the Right and the Party of the Left, whatever their actual name may be at any given time.*

Two other suggestions which are made from time to time also deserve a brief comment. It is sometimes argued that, after all, the differences between the two parties are not insuperable and that a 'Ministry of all the talents', a Government made up of the best men of all parties, pulling together in the national interest, would be the best solution for the country's difficulties (and countries are always in difficulties!). In fact,

* Bassett, *Essentials of Parliamentary Democracy*, pp. 58–9. The existence of a sizeable Liberal Party does not invalidate this argument. It is clearly, in these terms, a party of the Left, a party of change.

except in times of national emergency such as war, when the need for survival dictates Government policy, there are deep-rooted differences in outlook between the parties, however much they may shade into each other at the centre. The fundamental principle at issue has been identified by Professor Beer as 'the Tory belief in economic and social inequality'. There is, therefore, little likelihood that a coalition —excepting in times of national crisis—could be lasting. Furthermore, if both major parties joined to form a Government, there could be no strong Opposition, no real alternative Government, and the country would be well on the way to a one-party state. When we complain of factitious warfare between the parties, we should remember the alternatives:

> For us . . . the right to choose a government is inseparable from the right to dismiss it—and this we cannot do unless we have the right to organise more than one political party. This seemingly innocuous 'right' is denied to half the human race. The Communists justify this denial on the grounds that political parties represent class interests and that a Communist state, which knows only one class, needs only one party. If this were true it would mean that no one in a Communist country would feel the impluse to organise a second party. Yet the laws against this non-existent impulse are strict and the penalties for doing what nobody would want to do are extreme. On the whole, we may assume that the absence of an alternative party, in any society, means the presence of tyranny.*

The other suggestion sometimes made is that the Government should be composed of 'ten wise men' who would be above the party struggle and without party affiliations. This idea raises similar objections, is completely foreign to our constitution, and is inherently undemocratic. It is never made clear how the wise men would be chosen, nor how they would perpetuate themselves, but any conceivable method would involve the suppression of the people's right of election.

* Herbert Agar, *The Perils of Democracy*, (A Background Book) 1965, pp. 53–4. (The exceptional circumstances of developing countries are discussed on pp. 137–141.)

In eighteenth-century England the forum for the supreme struggle for power—the formation of an administration—was the House of Commons itself. As opinion shifted and groups changed their allegiance within the House, Governments were changed *between* elections rather than *at* elections. In modern times the forum for the choice of Prime Minister is a General Election, and a governing party which has lost at the polls does not await defeat in the House of Commons before resigning and advising the Sovereign to invite the leader of the erstwhile Opposition to form a Government. The outcome of the struggle for power between the parties is decided by the people; but once the election is over the struggle between the parties is continued within the Commons. We must now follow the course of the struggle there, and return to the subject raised in the last chapter: what checks are there on a majority party in the exercise of power?

Mr R. A. (now Lord) Butler rather startled some of those listening to him in the House of Commons when he declared, during the course of a debate on Procedure, 'We are here in a struggle for power'. As the Conservative Party had, at the time, a majority of over 50 Mr Butler's remark may have seemed rather far-fetched. Under normal circumstances perhaps it was: one party is usually elected, like the Labour Party in 1966, with a clear majority over all other parties, and the Opposition cannot hope to dislodge it from the seat of government for several years, barring a split in the ruling party or a national crisis. But circumstances are not always normal: it would not be fanciful to say that the Labour Government of 1950 was 'brought down' because it could no longer count on its position in the Commons, and the narrow majority won by Mr Harold Wilson in 1964 was clearly a major factor in his decision to call another General Election after only 17 months in office.

However, generally speaking, the victorious party at a General Election can count on a reasonable period in power. The duty of the Government is clear: to govern according to its interpretation of the best interests of the nation as a whole and to carry out the policies on which it was elected. The parliamentary duty of the Opposition is to oppose the Government on matters where the parties are divided and to criticise real or alleged shortcomings in, or omissions from, the Government's actions. These Opposition functions are recognised to be so important, indeed vital, in a representative democracy organised on party lines, that for well over a century the principal opposition party has enjoyed the title *Her Majesty's* Opposition, and the Ministers of the Crown Act, 1937, recognised the Leader of the Opposition's definite place within the constitution by awarding him a special salary, paid, like those of judges, out of the Consolidated Fund and so not subject to annual vote in the House. The Ministerial Salaries Act, 1965, has gone even further: the Leader of the Opposition in the House of Lords and the Chief Opposition Whips in both Houses (whose task it is so to organise their forces as to bring down the Government!) also now receive official salaries. The official Opposition is at all times two things: firstly, it is the chief watchdog and critic of the Government, extremely quick to pounce on any abuse of power; and secondly it is the alternative Government that the electorate can turn to at the next election, if it so chooses.

But surely, it may be asked, the Opposition is really powerless in the periods between elections? Is not the Government normally secure in its majority for five years *to do what it likes*?

This is far from the true position. The checks on a political majority's power take two forms: one is represented by the activities of critics inside Parliament, and the other is exercised by—or is latent in—the nation as a whole. The parliamentary checks on the Government's power may be dealt with first. It is true enough that any Government with a comfortable majority in the Commons (which may be taken as 25 or more seats) could *in theory* enact all its proposals without any heed to criticism, accepting no amendment and making no concessions. In practice, this happens very seldom. To show in detail how legislation is criticised, amended, re-drafted, sometimes withdrawn and very frequently substantially altered in its passage through Parliament would require a careful examination of the progress of a number of major proposals, from the publication of the original White Paper (or statement of the Government's intentions) to the first printing of a Bill, through debates in both Houses, the successive printings of the Bill as amended in each House after detailed scrutiny in committee, and so to the final publication of the Act.

A Government will seldom give way over some major plank of party policy, but on the details of a Bill—and Bills are usually very detailed documents—it is bound to be swayed by any cogently-argued criticisms. The criticism is supplied by the Opposition, by the backbench Government supporters and by the House of Lords. On occasions, of course, Governments reject any compromise. The old Secretary of the Treasury that Bagehot mentions has his descendants in the Whips' Office to-day: 'This is a bad case, an indefensible case. We must apply our *majority* to this question.'*

Criticism inside Parliament is more effective if it is backed by a strong current of feeling in the people as a whole (or in a sufficiently articulate section of the people). For it is—as is democratically proper—the electorate that provides the decisive check on a Government's actions. To begin with, the parties must periodically submit themselves to the judgment of the people in a General Election. This has led to the gibe that the British people are only sovereign once every five years, and for the rest of the time they are slaves. In fact, Government (and Opposition) are sensitive to the movement of public opinion all the time. A succession of reverses in by-elections, a prolonged unfavourable swing in the public opinion polls, sustained public agitation—these can all have the most profound effect on a Government's actions and future policies. The Government can never entirely forget

* *The English Constitution*, Fontana Library edition, p. 157.

the next General Election, when its success or failure will depend largely on its record in office.

A few examples of the pressures brought to bear on Governments by public opinion (usually made vocal in the House by the official Opposition and/or Government back-benchers) may be worth more than dogmatic statements. (Politics are not simple, and it is not suggested that in the examples given these were the *only* factors involved.) The Government's armed intervention in the Suez Canal crisis in 1956 aroused intensely strong feelings, and public opinion undoubtedly influenced the subsequent conduct of British policy. Sir Ivor Jennings has commented in *Cabinet Government*, 'The effect of public opinion on a democratic government was made more evident by the contemporary inability of opinion, national or international, to interfere with the intervention of the Soviet Union in the internal affairs of Hungary'. The operation of the 1957 Rent Act was not extended by ministerial orders as was first proposed. It was originally intended, in the reorganisation of London government, to break up the London County Council education authority, but this decision was reversed after a successful campaign by teachers, parents and officials in the area concerned. The 1965 White Paper on Commonwealth Immigration was strongly shaped by public opinion on that issue. And so examples could be endlessly multiplied. This is merely to touch on a very large and complex subject. Public opinion can only hope to influence a Government if it has a reasonable case and if it is supported by numbers. Vociferous extremist groups will never persuade a British Government to perse-cute the Jews. Agitation from the political Left for a ban on the sale of arms to South Africa did not sway a Conservative Government, which probably judged that most people did not feel strongly on the issue. Governments are particularly sensi-tive to criticism from their own supporters.

There can be no doubt of the power of the people to in-fluence Governments. But 'public opinion' may be wrong, and it is, indeed, a distinct danger in a democracy that Governments will become too timid and will shrink from necessary but unpopular steps. (It is already the case that Governments endeavour, if circumstances allow, to enact their unpopular measures in their first years of office and to provide more popular policies in the period preceding the next General Election.) The problem has been put in extreme form by Walter Lippman (quoted in Agar's *Perils of Democracy*, p. 51):

> Merely to enfranchise the voters, even to give them a true representation, will not in itself establish self-government; it may just as well lead, and in most countries has in fact led, to a new form of absolute state, a self-perpetuating oligarchy and an uncontrollable bureaucracy which governs by courting, cajoling, corrupting and coercing the sovereign but incompetent people.

This is a genuine dilemma, but inescapable so long as the people have ultimate power over Governments. The remedies, of course, are for the people to have a clearer perception of the national interest and for their elected representatives to offer responsible leadership. The first remedy should be the fruit of improvements in education; and for the second, on day-to-day issues Governments can defend unpopular policies on grounds of necessity and can hope to win over, by reasoned argument and persuasion, the majority of the electors to their case. As Herbert Morrison put it when introducing a Representation of the People Bill in 1944:

> Parliament itself cannot be expected to be at its best unless it is elected and kept under intelligent observation by an informed, upright, lively electorate. The people no less than Members of Parliament, perhaps even more than Members of Parliament, are essential to the success of our British democracy.

The 'public opinion' we have been discussing is an amorphous and volatile thing, difficult to pin down and define. It is expressed in many ways: in talk in pubs, in mass meetings, letters to editors, but above all in, through and by

59

Members of Parliament. It is very easy for Governments and the senior members thereof to become rather remote from the public, but the back-bench MP is always in touch with the governed—directly, and through his local party organisation, his local 'surgery,' his daily post. Public opinion is voiced most strongly through the public's elected representatives: on the Opposition side often vociferously; on the Government side more discreetly.

'Government back-bench revolts' are a common occurrence, and rightly, though most of them never reach the headlines. The Opposition may protest in the House at Question time: 'Is the Government aware of the penury in which the majority of our old people are compelled to live?' The Government back-bencher will catch a Whip or a minister in the corridors and say: 'You know, we must do something about the old-age pension. There's real hardship and a lot of feeling about it.' This is the Member's representative function, and he carries it out whether he agrees with all the opinions he collects or not.

This voicing by a Member of the doubts or troubles of his constituents, whether on the floor of the House or in private conversation, constitutes that essential meeting between the people and the Government for which Parliament exists. The influence of both the Opposition and the private Member is an essential aspect, often unnoticed, of the struggle for power. That influence relies for its force on its reflection of feeling in the nation at large.

In discussing the relationship between Members and the Government, and the people and the Government, we have, although indirectly, said most of what needs to be said here about the Cabinet, for the Cabinet is simply the senior direction of the Government. It is not chosen by the people. Indeed, some of its members—for the Lord Chancellor at least will have his seat in the House of Lords—are not even elected by the people. But because it depends for its survival on a majority in the Commons, and because that majority depends on the people's vote, its power too finds its basis in the will of the people. However, in discussing the struggle for power, a word should be said about the relationship of Cabinet and Parliament as a whole, and also about the special position of the Prime Minister. Both these matters have been much discussed recently, and with a good deal of misunderstanding.

The tendency of recent criticism has been to say that the power of the Cabinet has increased in relation to Parliament and that one object of parliamentary reform should be to give the House of Commons increased authority *vis-à-vis* the Government and the Cabinet. The objection to this line of argument is that Parliament and the Cabinet are not rivals, each fighting for a share of executive power: the Cabinet gathers into its hands *all* the executive powers needed to govern the nation, and its power has increased so greatly in the last century because central government has assumed a continually greater role in the affairs of the nation and the lives of every citizen.

Confusion arises because members of the administration (including, at the top, the Cabinet) are drawn from Parliament; but the function of those members of Parliament—peers and commoners—who are not members of the administration is not to attempt to *share* the Government's executive powers, but to support or criticise the policies put before them, as they are elected to do. The Cabinet is answerable to Parliament—and through Parliament to the nation—but it cannot delegate any of its powers.* What is needed is a strong Cabinet *and* a strong Parliament. Complaints about the Cabinet's powers come mainly from those in Opposition, which is natural enough, and from back-benchers on the ministerial side of the House who perhaps would like to share more fully in the process of government. Although it would theoretically

* The proposals for specialist committees of the Commons—with, if necessary, power to cross-question ministers—have no constitutional difficulties so long as they confine themselves to investigation, criticism and recommendation; but difficulty would probably arise immediately if they tried to share in the formulation of policy.

be possible to make all Government supporters members of the administration, this would be in practice an abuse of patronage, would stifle an important representative element and impair Parliament's critical function. Nearly 100 Members on the Government side of the House are in the administration and this seems to be quite enough. Parliament may need strengthening in its ability to examine, scrutinise and deliberate on the vast range of a modern Government's actions, but it is only the Government that can govern.

The popular identification of 'Parliament' with 'the Government' is a fruitful source of confusion. The two are separate even though the Government is in Parliament and even though it is subject to parliamentary control. What 'parliamentary control' means has been discussed by Professor Crick in his book *The Reform of Parliament* (p. 77): 'Control means *influence*, not direct power; *advice*, not command; *criticism*, not obstruction; *scrutiny*, not initiation; and *publicity*, not secrecy'.

The classic statement of the Prime Minister's position within the Cabinet is that he is the first among equals. He is a good deal more than this because he has two powers that belong to himself: the appointment (and dismissal) of ministers, and the power of asking the Queen to dissolve Parliament. These two powers alone ensure the Prime Minister his dominance over the ruling party, but to assume that he has therefore the free hand of a dictator would be quite wrong. His aim is to ensure that he—or his party—remains in power and he is therefore sensitive to all the forces of public opinion and of criticism in the two Houses that we have referred to earlier. He has also to consider his position in his own party and, especially, he is always conscious of the need to maintain the loyalty of his supporters in the Commons.

It must not be forgotten that the Premier is not directly elected by the people, but is chosen as leader by his party— and the party can change its leader (which means, if it is in office, the Prime Minister) without any appeal to the electorate. It is the party which checks the power of the Prime Minister. This has been demonstrated several times in recent years: the classic instance is the fall of Mr Neville Chamberlain in May 1940, when 33 of his regular supporters voted against him and some 60 abstained at the conclusion of the debate on the Norwegian campaign. But loss of confidence is not usually expressed so dramatically on the floor of the House: political parties are always fearful that any signs of dissension or any glimpses of 'washing dirty linen in public' will fatally damage their electoral prospects.

Nothing succeeds like success, but when things begin to go wrong, the Premier becomes vulnerable: Sir Anthony Eden resigned in January 1957 after an uneasy period in office (in 1956 he had been forced to take the unprecedented step of announcing to the press that he did not intend to resign) primarily because he lost the confidence of his party by his handling of the Suez affair. Mr Macmillan appeared to demonstrate conclusively in July 1962 the vast personal powers of the modern Premier when he dismissed from office seven Cabinet and nine other ministers; but this move increased rather than stilled the criticism of his leadership, justified or otherwise, within the party. Unrest had been growing ever since the breakdown of Britain's application to join the Common Market, a policy which the Prime Minister had adopted as particularly his own. Further difficulties—such as the Profumo affair—made his position still weaker, and he resigned in October 1963. (The immediate cause of both Sir Anthony's and Mr Macmillan's resignations was ill-health, which may well have dictated the timing of their leaving office.)

If the party can bring about the downfall of the Premier, it also circumscribes his exercise of his unique powers. No Premier is entirely free in forming an administration: while a primary consideration will be the ability of his colleagues, the Prime Minister will also be careful to balance the different elements in the party. Mr Wilson's ministry of October 1964 was a judicious mixture of right-wing and left-wing, trades unionist and intellectual, Gaitskellite and Bevanite, those who had helped Mr Wilson in his rise to the leadership and those who had carved out strong individual claims for themselves. A similar analysis could be made of all Cabinets. Further, in recommending a dissolution the Prime Minister's intention is to secure a victorious majority, and before taking this crucial step he will gather all the advice he can, particularly that which reaches him from the party machinery in the country.

None of this is intended to imply that the Prime Minister's powers in normal circumstances are not enormous and, indeed, open to abuse. Parliamentary government depends in part on a free discussion of issues; if government operates in secrecy there can be no parliamentary control and no proper judgment by the people. Some matters are of necessity secret—no one expects a Select Committee to investigate the efficiency of M.I.5—but if free debate on matters of national policy is stifled great harm is done to any democratic parliamentary system. The Rt. Hon. R. H. S. Crossman, in his Introduction to Bagehot's *English Constitution*, has referred to two crucial decisions taken by British Prime Ministers since the war in the secrecy of a small Cabinet group: one was the initiation of the development of British nuclear weapons by Mr Attlee's Government, and the other was Sir Anthony Eden's plans for an Anglo-French attack on Port Said in 1956. Mr Crossman says that the latter decision was taken 'without Cabinet consultation, and with the assistance of only a handful of his colleagues and permanent advisers', and he regards these two instances as supporting the thesis that to-day we have not parliamentary but 'Prime Ministerial' government.

But a very different lesson can be drawn from the secrecy in which these two steps were taken: they were both—there is no doubt—a blow to the democratic idea of consultation, debate, decision and action; but what is in a way paradoxically rather reassuring is that both these decisions have brought a long train of difficulties, argument and unexpected consequences in their wake. Both episodes were aberrations from the path of parliamentary government, not the heralds of a new norm.

We have tried to describe in this chapter the way in which supreme power—the power of central government—is distributed, shared, checked, limited, restrained or lost within the framework of the parliamentary system. It is sometimes objected that such an account as this ignores the *realities* of power for its forms: that real power is in the hands of government departments, nationalised industries, and so on, which work on—mostly in secret—more or less uncontrolled by their supposed masters. It is quite true that the day-to-day administration of a large country and the management of its economy are carried on in this way. But the essential point is that at any time the smallest irregularity can be raised in either House and may engage the full attention of the Minister responsible; and that all new departures in policy—many of which will, indeed, be suggested from within the departments—become the responsibility of the Minister and of the administration as a whole once adopted, and are then open to criticism and debate in Parliament, in the press, on radio and television.

The distribution of power in a modern state is too complex to be shown in a neat diagram in a constitutional handbook. So long as free men remain different from one another, with divergent interests and aspirations, the struggle for power will remain. Only authoritarian régimes can suppress this natural conflict. We do not suggest that parliamentary democracy can serenely harmonise and adjust all political differences, or that after free debate everyone will eventually reach agreement. On the contrary, Parliaments recognise the existence of conflict. They are, to use an ugly word, a device for institutionalising and civilising opposing views in the body politic. We shape our institutions and they shape us: generations have been brought up to appreciate the verbal battles in the Commons as a better form of argument than fighting in the streets. On major issues of policy, Governments refuse to compromise, and use their majority to enforce their will. On minor matters they are prepared to make concessions, and the willingness to grant them is strengthened by the knowledge that the other party may soon be in the Government's place and in a position to grant or withhold concessions in its turn. Parties, when they come to form a Government, accept in practice many measures they had bitterly fought when in Opposition (thus the acceptance by the Conservatives after 1951 of all the nationalised industries except for steel and road haulage, and the retention by Labour after 1964 of strict control on Commonwealth immigration). Governments do not, in fact, spend much of their time repealing legislation passed by the other party, although the occasions when they do so are well publicised.

The terms in which the struggle for power is carried on are vital. Mr Aneurin Bevan in a speech at Manchester in 1948 said: 'In my early life I had to live on the earnings of an elder sister and was told to emigrate. That is why no amount of cajolery and no attempt at ethical or social seduction can eradicate from my heart a deep burning hatred for the Tory Party that inflicted those bitter experiences on me. So far as I am concerned they are lower than vermin'. (Vincent Brome, *Aneurin Bevan*, p. 189.) It is perhaps not impossible to understand Bevan's personal use of the last phrase, but it is hard to forgive it. It immediately became famous because everyone instinctively recognised that it was an outrage against the tradition of English political discourse. (It would not, of course, have been in order in the House of Commons!) What one does with vermin is exterminate them, but this is not what the English do with their political opponents: they are 'the honourable Members on the opposite side of the House.' The majority, as Sir Ivor Jennings has put it, 'does not override the minority roughshod, because the habits of centuries have created a free people, disliking oppression even of minorities'.

While Senator Joseph McCarthy was unearthing the Communists in the US State Department, Arthur Miller wrote a play on a kindred theme: the witch-hunt at Salem, Massachusetts, in the seventeenth century. His notes to *The Crucible* refer obliquely to the civilising influence that has been exerted by our long parliamentary tradition:

> At this writing, only England has held back before the temptations of contemporary diabolism. In the countries of the Communist ideology all resistance of any import is linked to the totally malign capitalist succubi, and in America any man who is not reactionary in his views is open to the charge of alliance with the Red hell. Political opposition, thereby, is given an inhuman overlay which then justifies the abrogation of all normally applied customs of civilised intercourse. A political policy is equated with diabolical malevolence. Once such an equation is effectively made, society becomes a congeries of plots and counterplots, and the main role of government changes from that of the arbiter to that of the scourge of God.

Perhaps the English learned to fear the idea of 'Godly-thorough-Reformation' in politics in the seventeenth century. Since that time the political conflicts in society have been largely channelled into Parliament. The struggle for power is not confined to Parliament, but all the strands meet there. On some historic occasions, such as when the division bells rang on May 8, 1940, it is itself the scene of the struggle. More usually it is the forum where those who exercise power —on behalf of the majority—meet those who represent everyone. It is the place of accountability.

Further Reading

Sir Ivor Jennings: *Cabinet Government*, 3rd edn., Cambridge University Press, 1959.

R. T. McKenzie: *British Political Parties*, 2nd edn., Heinemann, 1963.

J. P. Mackintosh: *The British Cabinet*, Stevens, 1962.

R. Rose: *Politics in England*, Faber & Faber, 1965.

H. V. Wiseman: *Parliament and the Executive: An Analysis with Readings*, Routledge & Kegan Paul, 1966.

5
Honourable Members

THE TWO major parties, as we have already seen, have a dominating position at General Elections. Although there is still a sizeable Liberal vote, candidates of minor parties have only a small chance of election and Independents virtually none. In 1959 one Independent (Sir David Robertson) was elected, but this was rather a special case in that Sir David had previously been elected as a Conservative, had resigned from the party on one specific issue and was not opposed by an official Conservative candidate. At the 1964 and 1966 elections no Independents were elected.

The fact that every Member has a party label has been lamented by some writers. For example, Dr Ross wrote of the House of Commons elected in 1950 that it 'was something quite new in the history of this country in that (apart from the two absentee Irish Nationalists and, of course, the Speaker) every member was elected as the nominee or protégé of a major political party, and all but the nine Liberals were tied to either the Conservative party or the Labour party. It had less variety of membership, was more purely a major-party House, and had less freedom of opinion, than any of its predecessors down the centuries'.*

The elimination of Independents was, in fact, not a new thing at all: in the four General Elections between 1900 and December 1910 all the Members returned were either Conservative, Liberal, Labour or Irish Nationalist. In modern times Independents have always been few and far between and it was only in 1945 that genuine Independents (that is, those who defeated both Labour and Conservative opponents) reached double figures; a number of these were returned for

* *Elections and Electors*, p. 381.

the University seats where voters could enjoy, as it were, the luxury of voting for a party candidate in their local constituency and for a non-party candidate in the University seat.

The party chiefs would probably say that there are enough independents *within* the major parties! The very real difficulty is that however desirable a sprinkling of Independent Members may be it is very hard to think of any electoral system which would allow their election yet still preserve the strength of two major parties which is essential for our system of government. In theory, eminent persons of no party can make a useful contribution to Parliament in the House of Lords. In practice, however, although some appointments of this kind are made, the majority of peerages are awarded to party supporters. (See also pp. 120–122 below.)

Entry to the House of Commons is controlled by party. Without party support the prospects of election are negligible. Further, the majority of seats are 'safe' for one of the major parties. 'In two-thirds of constituencies, at the very least, the outcome in normal times is beyond doubt.' It follows, therefore, that 'most MPs are selected, not elected'.* The people elect the candidate, but the parties have chosen him. The decisive moment in the choice of the MP to represent Barnsley or Beckenham is not the election but the occasion when the constituency party adopts its prospective parliamentary candidate.

The procedure of the national parties in the selection of candidates differs in detail but is broadly similar in effect. If the sitting Member offers himself for re-election he will usually be re-adopted as candidate without much discussion, but if a new prospective candidate is required and the seat is either 'safe' or, at least, winnable, the local party may receive up to a hundred applications from would-be candidates. Even where the seat is likely to be lost the local party can expect to have a number of names to consider, for aspiring politicians

* Butler and King: *The British General Election of 1964*, p. 230.

realise that an unsuccessful but well-fought campaign may be a stepping-stone to an easier constituency.

A selection committee of the local party examines the applications and short-lists perhaps a dozen candidates who will be interviewed; it then recommends about three names to go before the executive council of the local association and the prospective candidate is selected after further interviews. The choice of candidate must next be ratified by a general meeting of the local association and approved by the national headquarters of the party.* Although in both Conservative and Labour Parties the national headquarters has the power of veto over the choice of candidate (a power which is very rarely used), local associations cherish their right to choose their own candidates and have often embarrassed their parties by refusing to accept a candidate pressed on them by the central office. A seat can usually be found for a Cabinet Minister not already in the House, such as Mr Bevin in 1940 or Mr Cousins in 1964, but a number of prominent Members who have been defeated at the polls have found it very difficult to secure adoption elsewhere, however much their party leaders may wish to see them back in the House.

The only certain thing about parliamentary candidates and Members is their variety: studies have been made of their age, occupation, education, religion and so on, but it remains impossible to generalise about the candidates of a single party, let alone candidates as a whole. There are, of course, certain broad trends, such as the far greater number of Conservative Members, compared with Labour, who went to public schools. The Nuffield studies of each General Election since the war have published useful tables of Members' occupations, and Andrew Roth has charted Members' connections with business, industry and the professions in his *Business Background of M Ps.*

* The practice described is that of the Conservative Party. A detailed study of the selection of candidates has been made by Austin Ranney: *Pathways to Parliament,* 1965.

These studies do not completely reveal, however, how many Members are now what may be called 'professional politicians', or full-time Members, and how many continue to pursue their original occupations after being elected. It is obvious that some occupations cannot be combined with Membership of the House of Commons: it is impossible to continue as a school-teacher or a miner or skilled worker in any other trade after election to the House of Commons. On the other hand, the practice of the law, company direction, journalism or trades union organisation are occupations which can be combined with service in Parliament. There is no question that if all Members were virtually forced, on election, to sever all connection with their previous occupation the House would be deprived of the services of many valuable representatives; at the same time the needs of the House require the full-time services of a large number of Members and as the work of the House becomes both more complex and more wide-ranging this need increases.

The number of 'professional politicians' is of necessity growing and, of course, Members who hope to rise high in the service of their party and the country have always tended to devote all their energies to their political careers. At a rough estimate about half of the 630 MPs are 'full-time' in the sense that they devote very little or no time to any other gainful occupation.

Until the end of the nineteenth century, Members on both sides of the House tended to be men of some means—indeed it was only in 1858 that the property qualification was repealed. A new state of affairs was created by the advent of the working-class MP who had no private income and who depended, perhaps, on the Labour Party's parliamentary fund which allowed elected Members a salary of £200 a year. It is still true—though only as a generalisation—that Conservative Members are on the whole better off than Labour MPs: more of them enjoy a source of income which supplements their pay as an MP. This may come from one of the professions, such as the law, from various kinds of business activity, from farming, from an armed services pension or from private means. Nevertheless, just as there are a number of wealthy individuals on the Labour benches so there are a number of Conservatives who have few resources other than their parliamentary salary. The wide discrepancy in the financial means of Members is only one of the factors that has made the question of their payment such a difficult one.

The tradition that MPs ought, as Sir Ivor Jennings put it, 'to be persons who could pay for the privilege and did not need to earn their living' broke down, as we have mentioned, with the arrival at Westminster in the later nineteenth century of Liberal and, later, Labour working-class Members. The Chartists had demanded payment of Members in the 1830s as part of their plan for securing working-class representation, but it was only adopted as Government policy in 1910. A resolution was passed by the House on August 14, 1911, providing for a salary of £400 a year for all Members other than Ministers. The principal argument employed by Lloyd George, who proposed the resolution, was that membership of the House should become more representative of the nation as a whole, and that the sum proposed was 'the minimum allowance to enable men to come here, men who would render incalculable service to the state and whom it is an incalculable loss to the state not to have here, but who cannot be here because their means do not allow it'.

In spite of the transparent force of this argument there was a good deal of opposition to the proposal on the grounds that the reputation of the House would be lowered, that Members would become professional politicians, or that their independence would be compromised. These criticisms have been revived from time to time. There may be some truth in them, but clearly the overriding consideration is that Members perform an essential democratic function and that most of them would be unable to do so without a parliamentary salary. The argument against professional politicians reflects the background of a different and more amateurish age: the House

72

needs a growing proportion of professional politicians who will devote all their energies to their parliamentary duties; as Lloyd George said in proposing the resolution in 1911, 'A Member who does his duty to his constituents has very little time left for anything else.'

The fear expressed by Austen Chamberlain that the House of Commons would become 'divorced from the life, the industry and the commerce of the country' is now seen to be quite unfounded. Without parliamentary salaries it is probable that the House would now consist almost exclusively of lawyers, businessmen, journalists, trades union nominees and those with inherited wealth. The question of a Member's independence is more difficult, but it is at least as true to say that if there were no parliamentary salary, MPs would be more dependent on outside interests than they are now.

The problems and controversies that have arisen in connection with the payment of Members have stemmed not so much from the fact of payment as from the inadequacy of the amount—inadequacy, that is, for the majority of Members, for a large part of the difficulty has always been that some Members do not need to rely on their parliamentary salary. The sum of £400 remained unchanged until 1937 when it was raised to £600. Further increases followed in 1946 (£1,000), 1954 (when an allowance which amounted to about £280 was added), and 1957 (£1,750). All these increases had been decided by the Government of the day in consultation with other Members, but in 1963, when the sum fixed in 1957 had clearly become quite inadequate for those Members who had no other source of income, an independent Committee under the chairmanship of Sir Geoffrey Lawrence, QC, was appointed to consider the whole question of the remuneration of Members of both Houses and of Ministers. This impartial investigation* was undoubtedly extremely useful, and did much to forestall the criticism that Ministers and Members

* *Report of the Committee on the Remuneration of Ministers and Members of Parliament*, Cmnd.2516, November 1964.

were in the invidious position of fixing their own salaries, although of course it remained for the Government to decide what action to take on the Committee's recommendations.

The Committee's principal proposals were that ministerial salaries should be roughly doubled (the Government decided to implement only half the increases proposed) and that Members' salaries should be increased to £3,250. This figure was accepted by the Government and implemented. Combined with an improved pension plan for older Members with long service, this new scheme should solve—at least for the time being—the difficulties that had arisen in the 1950s and early 1960s. It should no longer be the case that Members are driven—whether they wish to or not and whether to the detriment of their parliamentary duties or not—to seek some supplementary source of income. Inadequate pension arrangements have had the recognised effect of making some older Members without any alternative resources reluctant to retire and make way for younger and more energetic representatives.

At the same time, it is impossible to suggest that a salary of £3,250, matched against the very heavy expenses incurred by Members in secretarial help, postage, subscriptions and the additional costs of living away from home for those whose constituencies are outside the London area, and measured against the level of salaries in outside employment, is so large as to attract those without political convictions or with no sense of public service. (The Lawrence Committee reckoned that current expenses averaged about £1,250 a year for each Member.) So assuming that present trends in living costs continue, the Committee's recommendations represent no more than yet another interim settlement. This is perhaps a pity.

The Committee considered the desirability of linking the salary of Members with that of a particular level in the Civil Service, as is the practice in France, so as to provide for automatic adjustment in the future without the need for periodical re-examination of the whole question. The Committee rejected the idea on three counts: firstly because 'there is no basis of comparison at all between the two types of service'. This is perfectly true, but if the Committee found that the correct figure for Members at a particular time is closely similar to that earned by a particular grade in the Civil Service, why should it not be agreed that it should remain at that comparative level? Secondly, the Committee argued that the remuneration of Members 'should be determined on its own' and 'should not enjoy any automatic built-in protection'. But there seems no reason why the broad level of remuneration should have to be re-determined every ten years or so, particularly when the Committee states that it can only be 'an act of subjective judgment'.

The argument that MPs ought to enjoy no automatic protection from the effects of inflation is more attractive, but in opposition to this it may be asked whether the Civil Service feels that it is fully protected; and it could also be said that fixed salaries in the past have been singularly unsuccessful in encouraging Governments and MPs to prevent inflation. The Committee's third argument is that 'any link between salaries of Members of the House and salaries in the Civil Service might involve the latter at times in political controversy'. This is a possibility, but in fact it seems more likely that the link would be forgotten or, if remembered, accepted as fair.

Any scheme of differential payments to Members was rejected as impossible 'even if it were intrinsically desirable'. It is difficult to quarrel with this decision, but it is interesting to note that there were two considerations exercising the Lawrence Committee here: one was that some Members were wealthier or had heavier parliamentary expenses than others. The Committee pointed out that this was the unavoidable result of the varied membership of the House. But the second consideration was whether some attempt should be made to 'assess the value of the difference between part-time and full-time service'. The Committee judged that this would be equally impossible. It is certainly absurd to think of an accountant measuring columns in *Hansard*, totting up attendances at Standing Committees, counting the number of letters sent to constituents or examining clocking-in cards: the value of a Member's work cannot be measured in any such quantitative way, although in both France and Canada deductions are made from MPs' salaries for non-attendance. The amount of time, however, which Members devote to their work as representatives does vary a great deal, and much of the opposition within the House to the payment of a salary sufficient for those with no other income has come from those who devote only part of their time to parliamentary duties.

The Committee asked Members in a questionnaire whether their remuneration should be regarded 'as being in recognition of full-time or of part-time service'. Many of the replies 'were to the effect that in present conditions, whatever may have been the case in the past, the salary should be regarded as a recognition of full-time service. On the other hand, a substantial number of replies disclosed a firm belief that the House would suffer considerably in the quality of its work if it consisted entirely of "full-time professional politicians" and thus lose the benefit of the counsel of those Members who spend some part of their time actively engaged in professions and occupations outside the House.' The principle of paying part-time members of public boards a lesser salary than that of full-time members is well established. The parliamentary salary is now a fairly substantial sum to pay to those who devote only a few hours a week to their parliamentary duties. If it is agreed that the House should consist of both types of Member could not a smaller salary be paid to those who declare themselves to be part-time? The reader must judge for himself.

Membership of the House of Commons is not a career in any normal sense of the term. There are, it is true, some Members with long periods of service: it is possible for someone in his late twenties to be adopted for a comparatively safe seat which he could reasonably expect to hold for perhaps 30 or even 40 years. But this pattern is quite exceptional. Very few Members enter the House for the first time in their twenties: the average age of Members on first election is in the forties. Length of service in the House is also much shorter than is commonly supposed: the Lawrence Committee stated that in recent decades it had been on average about 15 years. Only 59 of the Members elected in 1964 had been in the House before 1945, and after the 1966 election this number declined still further to 33.

Not only does entry to the House usually come comparatively late in life, but Membership is also hazardous and uncertain. No seat is entirely safe, as Nigel Nicolson's experience at Bournemouth showed. If a Member has not made any great reputation for himself he will find it difficult to return to the House after being defeated. Parliamentary life is also extremely hard for those not in good health, and a number of retirements have been forced on MPs whose constitutions were unable to stand up to the strain. Some are disappointed when they find that their early hopes and expectations of a place on the front benches are unlikely to be fulfilled, and others leave Parliament in order to devote themselves to other occupations. But not all new Members are consumed with the desire to be Prime Minister. Many recognise quite clearly that they are likely to remain on the back benches or achieve at most minor office. The valuable work that they can perform as private Members is sufficient reward for ordinary mortals.

Some aspects of a Member's duties are uncontroversial: once elected he is the representative of all the people in his constituency, and will deal on equal terms with individual grievances or difficulties without regard to a particular person's opinions or voting history. This sort of work has increased greatly since 1945 and, apart from their extensive correspondence, many Members hold regular 'surgeries' in their constituencies, where individuals can seek help with their particular problems. Where a Member finds it difficult to obtain redress for what appears to be a genuine grievance, he may pursue it by means of Questions in the House or in an adjournment debate, so long as ministerial responsibility is involved. The difficulty is that Members are not able to investigate the rights and wrongs of the matter themselves, and are ultimately forced to accept the Ministry's answer. The Ombudsman, or Parliamentary Commissioner, which the Government has now appointed may well remedy this defect: Members will in future be able to pass on to him* grievances concerning the actions of the central Government which appear to be justified or at least to merit examination. The Parliamentary Commissioner will then be able to carry out a full investigation of the case, with access to the department's records.

A number of the individual problems brought to MPs are the result of decisions by local authorities—in the fields of housing, planning, education, etc.—and there is at present usually little that the Member can do to help. The Parliamentary Commissioner too, as at present proposed, will be precluded from investigating these matters. However, the White Paper does suggest that 'in due course it may be desirable to consider extending the powers of the Commissioner to deal with complaints of the private citizen against the administrative actions of other public authorities'.†

A Member will also naturally take a close interest in matters which affect his constituency. One example must suffice. It is not often that a back-bencher is successful in single-handedly amending a Finance Bill, but Mr George Wigg, when sitting on the Opposition benches, brought off this feat in 1957 in the course of his duties as a good constituency Member. He moved a new clause and began his speech as follows:

Under section 27 of the Vehicles (Excise) Act, 1949, a tower wagon carries a considerably lower rate of Excise Duty than

* Or, as Mr Grimond has suggested, to *her*: 'What might be valuable is an Ombudswoman: one of those intolerable, interfering, persistent females we all know who is totally lacking in respect for pompous males or their carefully graded hierarchies and smothering sense of protocol'.

† *The Parliamentary Commissioner for Administration*, Cmnd.2767, October 1965.

78

an ordinary vehicle. In my constituency, a firm manufactures a tower wagon of a kind not covered by the 1949 Act. The manufacture of these tower wagons affords a comfortable livelihood to a considerable number of my constituents and is a tribute to their skills and a testimony to the ingenuity, engineering ability and enterprise of the firm that undertook its production.

Mr Wigg's advocacy melted the heart of the Treasury, his clause was accepted, and one trusts that the firm flourishes to this day.

In pleading the constituency point of view Members may be at odds with party policy, and it is the duty of the Government to consider the nation as a whole which balances the local MP's partisanship for the interests of his own area. The fact that 200 people will be aggrieved by the closure of a branch line, or that 10,000 men will have to find new employment because of the closure of a factory working on military aircraft, the possibility that the line of a new motorway will spoil a cherished view, all these 'constituency points' have to be balanced by the Government against national needs and policies designed to meet the general welfare. The Member, of course, also recognises this and only rarely carries his protests so far as to vote against his own party. He will do what he can by Questions and speeches on the floor of the House and by lobbying Ministers behind the scenes, but in the end, where there is conflict, local considerations must usually give way to national ones.

As well as constituency interests, a Member may represent —either formally or informally—other interests in the House. Members' former occupations indicate in a rough and ready way the interests most strongly represented. The many former school-teachers on the Labour benches will always, naturally, be especially concerned with educational policy and will tend to argue that education should be given a high priority in the claims on public expenditure. So too, the miners, lawyers, farmers and businessmen will be inclined to defend the interests of their former or concurrent occupations.

Pressure groups naturally study Members' backgrounds carefully and direct their propaganda accordingly. Such bodies as the Abortion Law Reform Association, the Council for the Preservation of Rural England or the British Medical Association will try to discover Members who are sympathetic to their aims and can support their cause in Parliament. In this way many MPs represent various interests in a quite informal way. There are also more formal arrangements. The trades unions sponsor about 150 MPs, which means that a union helps with a large proportion of election costs and makes an allowance to the elected Member to help with his parliamentary expenses. Normally, sponsored Members defend in Parliament the interests of the unions whose assistance they receive. Similarly, Members who have close connections with business or financial interests will work in support of those interests. There is generally nothing wrong or underhand in all this: one of the functions of Parliament is to act as the forum where diverse interests can argue their case and become reconciled—so far as is possible—in the interests of the community as a whole. Pressure groups do not, of course, work only or even mainly through Parliament. It is customary for Government departments to consult closely with interested parties at all stages. Draft legislation is often circulated for comment, and discussions go on continually behind the scenes. Formal pitched battles (or agreed truces) such as the yearly confrontation between the Ministry of Agriculture and the National Farmers' Union over the annual price review are an exception. In all these discussions, as in Parliament itself, it is the Government which has the last word: its unanswerable argument against pressure groups is that it alone has the duty of deciding the national interest.

The convention in the House of Commons is simply that any Member who has a direct financial interest in the matter under discussion should declare it if he speaks in debate; he is not precluded from voting on any question of public policy. This matter was raised in the House in July 1965 when a

Member complained that a speech by Mr Callaghan, the Chancellor of the Exchequer, was a breach of privilege. Mr Callaghan was reported as saying that 'he did not think of them as the Honourable Member for X, or Y or Z. "I look at them and say Investment Trusts, capital speculators, or that is the fellow who . . . makes profit on gilt-edge; I have almost forgotten their constituencies, but I shall never forget their interests. I wonder sometimes whom they represent? The constituents or their own or their friends' particular interests?"' In a letter to the Committee of Privileges, Mr Callaghan explained, 'I did not have it in mind . . . either to state or imply that hon. Members who possess interests are acting or were acting improperly in taking part in discussion on the Finance Bill. The only qualification is that such interests should be, as they were, openly acknowledged by the Members concerned'.

The more difficult and controversial questions are those concerned with a Member's freedom of action. There are three interlocking relationships to be considered here: the Member and his constituents, the Member and his local party association, and the Member and his party nationally. The classic statement of the Member's freedom to speak and act as he thinks best is that of Burke in his Speech to the Electors of Bristol of November 3, 1774:

> Certainly, Gentlemen, it ought to be the happiness and glory of a representative to live in the strictest union, the closest correspondence, and the most unreserved communication with his constituents. Their wishes ought to have great weight with him; their opinions high respect; their business unremitted attention. It is his duty to sacrifice his repose, his pleasure, his satisfactions, to theirs,—and above all, ever, and in all cases, to prefer their interest to his own.
>
> But his unbiased opinion, his mature judgment, his enlightened conscience, he ought not to sacrifice to you, to any man, or to any set of men living. These he does not derive from your pleasure,—no, nor from the law and the Constitution. They are a trust from Providence, for the abuse of which

he is deeply answerable. Your representative owes you, not his industry only, but his judgment; and he betrays, instead of serving you, if he sacrifices it to your opinion. . . .

To deliver an opinion is the right of all men; that of constituents is a weighty and respectable opinion, which a representative ought always to rejoice to hear, and which he ought always most seriously to consider. But *authoritative* instructions, *mandates* issued, which the member is bound blindly and implicitly to obey, to vote, and to argue for, though contrary to the clearest conviction of his judgment and conscience, —these are things utterly unknown to the laws of this land, and which arise from a fundamental mistake of the whole order and tenor of our Constitution.

Parliament is not a *congress* of ambassadors from different and hostile interests, which interests each must maintain, as an agent and advocate, against other agents and advocates; but Parliament is a *deliberative* assembly of *one* nation, with *one* interest, that of the whole—where not local purposes, not local prejudices, ought to guide, but the general good, resulting from the general reason of the whole. You choose a member, indeed; but when you have chosen him, he is not member of Bristol, but he is a member of *Parliament*.

Burke's argument has been repeated with approval on many occasions: it is quoted by every Member who at any time comes into conflict with his constituents or his party. But the argument used nowadays against a Member's right to form his own judgment is not that adopted in Burke's day. It is not so much, 'You are the Member for Bristol and should do whatever we tell you in support of our interests'; it is rather 'You were chosen by us [the local party association] and elected by the Labour or Conservative voters of this constituency to support the party whose candidate you were. You must support that party, otherwise we, the local association, will disown you'. It is conflict of this kind that is now a recurring feature of parliamentary representation.

The ultimate sanction against a Member's freedom of action in present times is expulsion from the party: for without party endorsement there is virtually no chance of re-election. The fate of the four Members expelled from the Labour party who stood as independent candidates at the 1950 election, and who all lost to officially-sponsored rival candidates, is sufficient proof of this. Expulsion from the party is rare, though it is less uncommon for the 'whip' to be temporarily withdrawn from dissident Labour MPs; a more frequent occurrence in both parties is that the Member finds himself in conflict with his local association, and this can have just as disastrous an effect on his prospects of retaining his parliamentary seat, although in many cases the conflict is resolved.

The military action at Suez in 1956 produced a crop of examples. Stanley Evans, Labour Member for Wednesbury, disagreed with his party's policy and was asked to resign by his divisional Labour Party. Although he would have been perfectly entitled to stand his ground and refuse to leave the Commons, Mr Evans complied with his local party's request. A number of Conservative MPs refused to support the Government's policy: Nigel Nicolson declined to resign his seat, but his local association adopted a new candidate for the next election; Sir Frank Medlicott was in conflict with his local association and announced that he would not stand at the next election; Anthony Nutting resigned his ministerial post as Minister of State for Foreign Affairs, and after his local party had demonstrated its support for the Prime Minister's policy, resigned his seat as well. On the other hand, the Handsworth Conservative Association issued a statement recognising the right of their Member, Sir Edward Boyle, who had also resigned from the Government in protest, to act in accordance with his convictions.

Instances of conflict between the local party and the Member are constantly occurring, but it is not often that such cases are pushed to a decisive issue.* Agreement to differ, at the least, is usually reached. A Member is normally

* Ranney, in *Pathways to Parliament*, p. 89, identifies in the Conservative Party 12 instances since 1945 in which constituency associations have denied MPs readoption. 'In four cases the association objected to their Members' defiant votes in Parliament but in eight they objected to the Members' personal inadequacies'.

allowed considerable latitude over issues which are commonly regarded as peculiarly matters of conscience, but they have far less freedom of action in other matters. If they question some basic party tenet they may expect a strong reaction from the local association. Obviously, this must be a matter of balance: a Member cannot expect complete freedom of action and opinion in the two-party system, but it would be intolerable if he were denied all exercise of his independent judgment by his local or national party bosses. Where there are only two major parties, each is bound to reflect a broad spectrum of opinion; the eccentric and the nonconformist must be allowed to exist within the party when he can no longer survive outside it. The thorns in the flesh of the party managers may only receive their due when they have ceased to cause trouble; but we must hope that the Conservative Party has more Churchills and the Labour Party more Bevans.

Membership of the House of Commons has been called 'the youngest profession'. Members *are* engaged in a profession: the profession of politics. The 630 individual MPs at Westminster are the backbone of parliamentary government. The quality of any Parliament depends on the calibre and vision—and sheer hard work—of its Members. No procedural reform could compensate for a lack of representatives with the essential qualities of political experience, initiative and expertise. More difficult still, our elected Members must preserve in the hothouse atmosphere of Westminster their humanity and their personal integrity. Bagehot, writing a hundred years ago, has vividly described the House of Commons as it still is even in the present age of party discipline:

> Every Member . . . has his own object (good or bad), his own purposes (great or petty); his own notions, such as they are, of what ought to be. There is a motley confluence of vigorous elements, but the result is one. . . . There is a 'feeling of the House,' a 'sense' of the House, and no one who knows anything of it can despise it. A very shrewd man of the world

went so far as to say that 'the House of Commons has more sense than anyone in it'.

Further Reading

W. L. Guttsman: *The British Political Elite*, MacGibbon & Kee, 1963.

Nigel Nicolson: *People and Parliament*, Weidenfeld & Nicolson, 1958.

P. G. Richards: *Honourable Members: a Study of the British Back-Bencher*, 2nd edn., Faber & Faber, 1964.

6
Westminster Workshop

BY A SORT of visual shorthand, a picture of the Manhattan skyline evokes in everyone's mind the thought of the United States; the idea of India is conjured up by the Taj Mahal, that of Russia by Lenin's tomb and Red Square, that of France by the Eiffel Tower. It is fitting that the universally accepted image of England should be the Palace of Westminster, for it is what has happened in that building—or in the huddle of buildings that preceded it on the same site in the years before the fire of 1834—that has shaped the history of England for hundreds of years. It says much for the relationship of people and Parliament that the English themselves accept the home of their legislature as the symbol of themselves and their country; it is closer to their hearts than Buckingham Palace or the offices of the Treasury.

Although the outline of this early Victorian monument of the Gothic revival is known to everyone, there are comparatively few who have visited the Palace, and those who have a detailed idea of the multifarious activities pursued within its walls are fewer still. This is a pity, for the public may freely wander through a good deal of the building on Saturdays and during parliamentary recesses. From the bottom of the Victoria Tower, the route taken by the Queen when she comes to open a new session may be followed through the Robing Room and the Royal Gallery to the Chamber of the House of Lords. Members of the public can then proceed (where the Queen may not go) towards the Central Lobby and the Chamber of the House of Commons—which always excites the exclamation 'But how small it is!'

St Stephen's Hall, the site of the old House of Commons, leads to the gloomy chill of Westminster Hall, the principal surviving remnant of the medieval Palace, which will be remembered by the thousands who filed past Sir Winston Churchill's catafalque in January 1965. When Parliament is sitting there is less opportunity for exploring at will, but a far more exciting atmosphere. Everyone, of course, has the right to come to the Central Lobby to seek an interview with his Member of Parliament, and the Chambers of both Houses have public galleries where the process of question, debate and decision can be seen in action.

In the mornings there will probably be one or more Standing Committees of the House of Commons working 'upstairs' on the Committee Corridor, considering the details of the Bill before them line by line and, sometimes, word by word. In another committee room a Private Bill, probably promoted by a local authority, may be under consideration, and witnesses will be examined and cross-examined by counsel for those promoting and opposing the bill. There is provision for the accommodation of the public in these rooms as there is in the Moses Room, near the Chamber of the House of Lords, where the Law Lords may be found hearing and ruling upon a case that has reached the final court of appeal.

Only a few historians and archivists are aware that the Victoria Tower is the repository for the records of Parliament; here, on 12 air-conditioned floors, are kept the original copies of the statutes, signed with the Royal assent, and a mass of other printed and manuscript material, dating back to 1497, which is available to the public in the Search Room of the House of Lords Record Office.

Although a diligent and properly inquisitive 'stranger' (as members of the public are called within the Palace) could spend several days exploring the public activities of Parliament, there is also a mass of business, equally essential to the workings of a Parliament, being carried on of necessity in private. Some of this must be mentioned because it is so important in itself for the proper functioning of Parliament and because many people make the strange assumption that when a Member is not speaking in the Chamber he must be doing nothing or, at the most, exchanging doubtful gossip in the smoking room. A number of these activities, as they might engage a back-bench Member of the Commons, will be touched on rather more fully in the next chapter.

Just as much of the detailed scrutiny of legislation is undertaken by Standing Committees, so much of the detailed work of the House in examining, criticising and commenting on the actions of the Government is undertaken by Select Committees of about 15 Members usually drawn from all three parties. These Committees take evidence from various witnesses on the subject of their inquiry and later publish a report with the transcript of all or some of the evidence which was heard. Select Committees meet in private in rooms on the Committee Corridor either in the morning, or, more usually, in the afternoon.

The Select Committee of Public Accounts is charged with the examination of Government expenditure, and it has the skilled assistance of the Comptroller and Auditor General and his staff. The chairman of the Committee is by tradition a senior Opposition Member. Where the Committee finds grounds for criticism, the Treasury and the departments concerned usually produce a reply to the Committee's observations and this is published with the Committee's report.

The Select Committee on Estimates has an abnormally large number of Members (43), and this enables it to divide its work among sub-committees, each of which (since 1965) concentrates on a particular sphere of Government activity: Technological and Scientific Affairs, Economic Affairs, Social Affairs, Defence and Overseas Affairs and Building and Natural Resources. At the beginning of the session each sub-committee chooses for examination a particular subject within its general field—in session 1965–66, for example, the sub-committee on Social Affairs chose the Police. Sub-committees have recently been given the power to employ temporary expert assistance to help them in their inquiries. The reports are frequently wide-ranging and contain a number of criticisms and suggestions. The range of the Estimates Committee's work is indicated by the titles of a few recent reports: The Board of Inland Revenue; Trooping; Classified Roads; H.M. Dockyards; The Home Office; The Forestry Commission; Military Expenditure Overseas. The Department's reply to each report is published, and if the Estimates Committee is not satisfied with the Executive's reaction to its recommendations, it will return to the attack and criticise the Department's observations. The Select Committee on Nationalised Industries is appointed to 'examine the Reports and Accounts of the Nationalised Industries established by Statute' and it normally devotes a whole session to the study of one of the industries, eventually producing a report containing a large number of recommendations and backed up by a mass of published evidence taken from officials of the industry concerned and from the responsible departments of the central Government. The Committee has been of the greatest value in informing Parliament and the public of the problems facing the nationalised industries, and in discussing the decisions that have to be taken in this sector of the economy. The Committee publishes at a later date the industry's observations on its report, and it has also published a 'follow-up' study to examine the effects of its recommendations. Substantial reports have been produced in the last few years on the Air Corporations, British Railways, the Gas Industry and London Transport.

Some of the more important reports of these Select Committees are debated in the House and altogether they form one of the principal weapons for parliamentary scrutiny of the actions of the central Government and of the publicly-owned industries. Another scrutinising committee is the Select Committee on Statutory Instruments which, with the professional assistance of the Speaker's Counsel, examines the mountain of delegated legislation made by ministers under powers given them in various statutes. Other important Select Committees—on Procedure, Privileges and House of Commons Services—are concerned with more domestic matters.

Select Committees of the House make considerable demands on Members' time, but they offer a fruitful field of work for back-benchers. Their labours may receive little notice in the press, but the whole spirit of central Government administration is influenced by the knowledge that it must be able to stand up to vigorous parliamentary investigation.

All these are official committees of the House of Commons and each is engaged in some essentially parliamentary activity. But during the parliamentary day there will also be a number of other committee meetings attended by varying numbers of Members. The most important of these are the party groups. As well as general meetings of the Conservative Private Members' Committee (usually called the '1922 Committee') and of the Parliamentary Labour Party, both the major parties have a large number of specialist committees. The 1922 Committee, for example, has a list of some 22 committees and 16 sub-committees. Members will join the various committees according to their interests and responsibilities, and all spheres of Government activity and legislation are covered: Health and Social Security, Education, Defence (with sub-committees for Army, Navy and Air Force), Agriculture (with sub-committees for Horticulture and Fisheries), Broadcasting, etc. The Parliamentary Labour Party has a similar list of specialist committees, and in addition Trades Union Members have their own group. When in Opposition the Parliamentary Labour Party also chooses a working party to deal with each major item in the Government's programme: this examines the legislative proposals in detail, co-ordinates contributions to debates in the House, drafts and tables amendments, and so on. The committee system within the parties is extremely flexible and new groups are quickly created to meet new developments. The pressure of work on the committees varies considerably: when, for instance, the Finance Bill is before the House, the Opposition party's Finance Committee will probably be meeting daily.

The propensity of the English to form themselves into committees, remarked on by so many rather puzzled observers, is still not exhausted. In addition to the party groups, there are a number of important unofficial all-party committees, of which probably the most influential is the Parliamentary and Scientific Committee, which brings together Members of all parties of both Houses and those working in science and technology. Its aim is 'to provide Members of Parliament with authoritative scientific and technological information in connection with debates and to ensure that proper regard is had for the scientific point of view'.

We have attempted no more than a bare outline of a few of the activities which Members of the House of Commons may be collectively pursuing in different rooms in the Palace, while all that meets the public eye may be a rather dreary discussion of the Rural Water Supplies and Sewerage Bill in a very thinly-attended House. Furthermore, we have not even mentioned the work which a Member performs on his own, as an individual. Some idea of this part of his day must be left to the next chapter.

Parliament is the meeting-place of Government and the representatives of the governed and, during the afternoon and evening, ministers, if not suffering indigestion at public dinners will probably spend more time in the Palace of Westminster than in their Departments. The minister may pass most of the evening in his room, ready to answer the summons of the division bell, working on his departmental files, meeting deputations from outside organisations, seeing formally or informally Members of all parties on matters within his responsibility, conferring with fellow-members of the Government and with officials of his own ministry. If the minister is in the Cabinet he will have an additional mass of paper to work through, and the privacy of his room within the Palace, while debate continues possibly into the early hours of the morning, may give him a useful opportunity to catch up.

Before looking at a Member's daily work in detail in the

next chapter, we must glance briefly at the invisible machinery of Parliament—at the organisation and staffing of those services and amenities which supply the needs of Members.

The control of the Palace of Westminster changed hands in April 1965. Until that date the Palace was under the control of the Lord Great Chamberlain who, when Parliament was sitting, leased, as it were, the area occupied by the House of Commons to the Serjeant-at-Arms, acting on behalf of Mr Speaker. At week-ends and during recesses, control reverted to the Lord Great Chamberlain. This rather odd system, where the principal law-making body was not even master in its own House, simply reflected the historical fact that the Commons was occupying part of a royal palace which had remained under the control of a high court functionary. With the agreement of the Queen, however, on April 26, 1965, the control, use and occupation of the Palace passed to the two Houses of Parliament, each House being given jurisdiction over the area it then occupied. (The small proportion of the Palace which is exclusively used by the monarch—such as the royal Robing Room—remains in the hands of the Lord Great Chamberlain.)

Thus, while the useful fiction that the Houses of Parliament are a royal palace is maintained—useful because it carries with it such tangible benefits as exemption from the licensing laws —the running of the accommodation and services of the House of Commons (the arrangements in the House of Lords are similar) is now vested in Mr Speaker on behalf of the House. A Select Committee on House of Commons Services advises Mr Speaker; and this powerful Committee has (at present) four sub-committees to deal respectively with catering, administrative matters, the Library, and the distribution and improvement of the accommodation of Members, staff and press. The new set-up owes much to the long campaign waged by Mr Charles Pannell from the Opposition backbenches. When he achieved office as Minister of Public Building and Works in 1964 he was well placed to help promote proposals he had championed for so long.

The people employed within the Palace are, broadly speaking, working for one of two distinct purposes: they are either supplying the needs of Members, or they are engaged in reporting Parliament to the people and the world outside.

The staff directly employed by the House of Commons (leaving out of account the catering staff and those employed by the Ministry of Public Building and Works on cleaning, heating and maintaining the fabric of the Palace) is comparatively small: including 45 part-time women cleaners it numbers about 320. The Department of the Clerk of the House is responsible for the conduct of business, for advising Members on procedural matters, for compiling the daily record of the transactions of the House, for staffing the Standing and Select Committees, and so on.

Mr Speaker has a small staff of his own and is also responsible for a group of offices. The Editor and staff of the Official Report produce *Hansard* which, in its daily published form, is the vital and verbatim record of debates. The Vote Office distributes *Hansard* and parliamentary papers to Members. The Fees Office is responsible for expenditure, including the payment of Members' salaries. The Library of the House was established in 1818, but its modern terms of reference—to supply Members as rapidly as possible with the most accurate, comprehensive and up-to-date factual information and research upon any subject connected with their parliamentary duties—date from 1946, when a Select Committee recommended important changes to make the Library a better instrument for the present-day needs of Members.

The Serjeant-at-Arms and the staff in his department maintain order in the Chamber, the public galleries, and the rest of the area occupied by the House of Commons and are concerned with the allocation of accommodation and all sorts of 'housekeeping' matters.

The direct cost of the House of Commons—excluding expenditure on the furniture and fabric of the building and on

Members' salaries—amounted in 1965–66 to an estimated £1,225,990, and of this more than £540,000 was for stationery and printing (Select Committee Report on the Palace of Westminster, H.C. 285 of session 1964–65, Appendix 3). The total cost of Parliament, including the House of Lords, Members' salaries (£2 million), expenditure on the heating, maintenance, etc., of the Palace of Westminster, is roughly £5½ million (Civil Estimates, 1966–67).

The late Sir Ivor Jennings, in his book on *Parliament*, wrote: 'the real function of the House [of Commons] is that which Bagehot broke up into three elements, to "express the mind of the people,", to "teach the nation what it does not know", and to make us "hear what otherwise we should not" '. Parliament now shares this function with media which did not exist in Bagehot's day—the mass-circulation newspaper, wireless and television—but direct communication between Parliament and people remains vital. It is a two-way traffic: we have already mentioned the ways in which 'the people' bring their influence to bear on Members. The other side of the coin is the persuasive and expressive force which Parliamentarians can embody in their speeches and actions. This is, perhaps, seen at its clearest and most vital in times of national crisis: Churchill's speeches in 1940–41 were felt to be the living embodiment of the national will to survive. At other times, where politics are concerned, Parliament remains a focus and a primary source of news for the other organs of communication.

The news of debates in the House of Commons begins its journey to the people in the reporters' gallery, above the Speaker's chair. The *Hansard* reporters take the copy for the full verbatim report of proceedings, which is rushed to the printer at intervals throughout the day, so that it can be printed and despatched by the next morning. Although there may be well over a hundred reporters in the gallery, the only others who take a full report of what Members say are those of the *Times* and the Press Association—apart from the

Times all the newspapers rely for the text of what is said in the House on the Press Association report, and their reporters in the gallery, although they may take down some important passages, are primarily there to watch proceedings, absorb the atmosphere of the House and write the 'sketch' which brings the bare bones of a transcript to life.

Only the *Times, Guardian, Daily Telegraph* and some of the leading provincial dailies regularly publish conscientiously summarised accounts of the day's proceeding in both Houses. The popular press may devote hardly any attention at all to a debate on a major—but uncontroversial—Bill. Nevertheless, it will usually contain a good deal of parliamentary reporting: answers to Questions and ministerial statements normally provide some good copy every day. Popular newspapers do not publish summaries of debates because most of their readers do not wish to read them. This is perfectly reasonable —many House of Commons debates are not worth reading in full, or even in summary, except by those with a political or other specialist interest in the subject, whatever it may be, under discussion; and for these there is *Hansard* or a 'serious' newspaper. But when, on a major issue that touches the lives of everyone, Members fulfil their role of 'expressing the mind of the people' and 'teaching the nation what it does not know', the newspapers—however self-consciously illiterate— do offer a reasonable summary of debates: this happened during the Suez crisis and during the Common Market negotiations.

The British Broadcasting Corporation and Independent Television News have automatic studios at Westminster from which they can transmit reports of debates for inclusion in their news bulletins.

Quite apart from the reports of speeches in the House, the Palace is the source of most of the political 'news' (a polite word for a mixture of hard facts and gossip, inspired rumours and pure speculation) that appears in the newspapers, the radio and television bulletins, and which is sent in agency messages all over the world. This commentary on the political scene is mainly the province of the Lobby correspondents. The journalists of this select band are allowed into the Members' Lobby just outside the Chamber of the House, and can there rub shoulders with MPs, Ministers and leading Members of the Opposition. As well as the information which they pick up in this way—('the Opposition will not divide the House at the end of the debate on...'; 'Mr Blank is generally popular with his back-bench supporters, but his critics suggest...')—they are also the privileged recipients of a good deal of exclusive briefing. The Lobby is, in fact, a most important channel of communication between politicians and the people; it is, perhaps, especially useful to the Government, who use it to prepare the ground for new developments. The following extract (taken at random as this chapter was written) from the *Guardian* of January 7, 1966, illustrates the work of the Lobby correspondent:

CABINET STAYS FIRM ON TASK OF PRODUCING ECONOMIC RECOVERY
By Francis Boyd
Our Political Correspondent

The Government is reviewing the effects of the financial restrictions imposed by Mr Callaghan in his attempts to strengthen sterling and correct the adverse balance of payments, and it will take any further measures it thinks necessary to secure these two objectives.

The question of an early election is said not to be diverting the Government from discharging the stern task it accepted in October 1964. . . .

The Chancellor reported to Mr Wilson earlier this week on the Treasury's prospects. . . . Ministers are well aware of the economic uncertainties of this year, but base their hopes of a successful outcome on two grounds. . . .

It remains to consider how well the Palace of Westminster measures up to its now fashionable description as a 'workshop'. An immense amount of work is done, but often in far from ideal conditions. One great difficulty is the Palace itself

—a building designed in an age when the sphere of parliamentary and governmental activity was much smaller than it is now, when most of the legislators were 'part-time', and when the urgency of public events was less pressing. A great deal has been done over the last ten years to make more rational use of the accommodation that is afforded in the Palace, and conversion and new building have been pressed forward wherever possible—the extensive wine cellarage originally installed under Mr Speaker's house has been used to provide more storage space for the Library, new rooms have been constructed in the roof space, and an entirely new building is arising in one of the courtyards.

Members have been furnished with desks and filing cabinets, and secretarial accommodation has been provided in the elegant building next to the Jewel Tower, across the road from the St Stephen's entrance. But the limit to what can be squeezed into the pint pot will soon be reached and a radical improvement in the workshop facilities of Members—which would surely include at least a private room for all Members who want one—must await the longer-term plans for a new parliamentary building in Bridge Street, opposite Big Ben. This has been promised, and if, before it is built, Members could reach a united view on their own requirements—for their opinions on these have been much divided in the past—the way would be clear to equip Parliament with the tools it needs to do its twentieth-century job.

Many frustrations have been suffered by those who have tried in the past to improve the resources of the back-bench Members. The matter is now—through the House of Commons Services Committee—under the control of Members themselves. The real or alleged obstructiveness of the Lord Great Chamberlain can no longer, as in the past, be offered as a whipping boy. 'It is not the mere existence of Parliament', said Sir Hugh Munro-Lucas-Tooth in a debate on October 27, 1965, 'which ensures our freedom but the way in which we do our job here. If Parliament becomes inefficient or impotent, the first thing which will suffer will be our personal freedom as citizens. I will not base my argument on the view that the power of the executive is too great. On the contrary, I recognise that the power of the executive is great and I believe that, whether we like it or not, it will grow greater. I do not see any help for that. I do not like it, but I think it quite inevitable. But if it is inevitable, then that is the best reason why we should ensure that we make the machinery for the supervision of the executive by Parliament as modern and as strong as it can be.'

Further Reading

P. Marsden: *The Officers of the Commons 1363–1965*, Barrie and Rockliff, 1966.

7

Interlude

A Day in the Life of an MP

To GIVE an idea of the parliamentary day we shall have to mingle fiction with fact. As neither *Hansard* nor any other printed record gives an adequate idea of what a Member of the House of Commons actually does, we will invent a 'hero' and outline a day's activities. Our aim is to indicate the possible scope and variety of a Member's work and of the proceedings in the House, and we cannot suggest that the day we describe is typical or 'average'—we rather hope indeed that no Member is ever quite so busy as our man, whom we will call Mr William Ember.

He is in his forties, a back-bench member of the party in opposition, and he first entered the House three years ago. He represents a mixed urban, rural and seaside constituency in Dorset, and still devotes part of his energies to the family timber-importing business, based on a small port within the constituency. He is a director of the firm along with his brother and two others.

Ember's working day begins over breakfast at the flat in Pimlico which he shares with an MP for a Scottish constituency. For both of them it is rather more than a *pied-à-terre* but less than a home. Ember is not happy to be separated from his wife and two children for most of the week, and they have agreed that when his children finish schooling, in a few years' time, and if he is still an MP (which is never certain!) the main family home will have to be moved to London.

As he breakfasts, he glances through the *Daily Express* and *Daily Mirror* and works rather more carefully through the *Guardian*, *Times* and *Financial Times*. Keeping abreast of the news and noting developments of interest to himself, his constituency and his party, is one of the most onerous of a Member's duties. The main home news is a report on the aircraft industry, which is of direct interest to Ember because one of the big companies has a subsidiary factory in his constituency. The matter is to be discussed at a party sub-committee the next day which Ember will attend.

Another article which catches his eye appears on the *Guardian*'s women's page. It says that although it is official policy to allow unrestricted visiting of children in hospital, a large number of hospitals still refuse, in practice, to allow it. This subject has interested Ember and his wife ever since one of their children, at an early age, had to go to hospital for a week. He remembers, as he reads the article, the various stages in the campaign to improve the welfare of children in hospital—the setting up of the Platt Committee of the Central Health Services Council, its recommendation (among many others) in favour of unrestricted visiting for parents, the Minister of Health's circular to hospitals which advised them to adopt the suggestions made by the Committee. He had thought that this particular battle was over, but now he resolves to draft a Parliamentary Question on the subject— something like 'Whether the Minister is satisfied with the progress that has been made in implementing the policy of allowing unrestricted visiting hours for parents of children in hospital; and whether he intends to issue any further advice to hospital boards.' Rather clumsy, he feels, but the Clerks in the Table Office may suggest a better wording. Ember mentally rehearses a Supplementary Question referring to the successful arrangements which have been made at the hospital in his constituency, and asking for pressure on hospitals to be kept up.

After absorbing the main news in the various papers, Ember turns to his copy of *Hansard*. He was not at Westminster the previous day because, as a member of one of the sub-committees of the Select Committee on Estimates, he was visiting the central office of the Ministry of Social Security situated at Newcastle-upon-Tyne, in the course of the sub-committee's inquiry into the work of the Ministry. He skims quickly through the speeches in the main debate—on foreign affairs, and he felt that he knew pretty well what every speaker would say—and then he reads through some of the Questions more carefully.

The newspapers give a lively and vivid account of a rumpus in the House during the Prime Minister's Questions—apparently a mock-solemn Question on when the Government would introduce legislation to abolish the House of Lords sparked off a good deal of hilarity and indignation—but the *Hansard* account seems disappointingly tame; the hubbub and interjections are all reduced to an occasional '(interruption)' or 'Hon. Members: No!' Ember hopes that if the proceedings in the House are ever televised these moments of light relief will still be possible.

At about 9.45 Ember drives to the Palace of Westminster. He collects his mail—he always gives his official address as 'The House of Commons' and so only receives personal letters at his flat—and takes it up to the room where he and two other back-benchers have desks. Ember has only the part-time services of a secretary, whom he shares with another Member, and he wishes that she had time to undertake a preliminary sorting of his post. Newsletters and duplicated hand-outs from the North Vietnam Liberation Front, the League against Cruel Sports, the Free Cuba Association, the Income Tax Payers' Society and about a dozen others go straight into the wastepaper basket. They may be important, but they aren't among Ember's particular concerns.

There are a number of letters with various postmarks in Ember's constituency, but first of all he opens the copy of the previous day's local newspaper which is regularly mailed to him. He finds, as he suspected he would, that there have been further developments in the saga of Fettlebridge, a small market town in his constituency which the Greater

London Council has selected as a possible site for a scheme under the Town Development Act. The G.L.C. has already entered into discussions with the urban district and county councils and proposes that the town be expanded from its present population of 6,000 to around 40,000 over the course of about five years. A number of London firms—including a fairly small but world-famous manufacturer of hypodermic needles—are interested in moving their businesses and their employees to Fettlebridge. Ember, who is a member of his party's New Towns Committee, is whole-heartedly behind the plan, but there is some strong local opposition. Ember feels sure that it is only a minority, but quite a powerful one.

The local paper has a long letter from a local Councillor, whom Ember knows quite well. He retired five years ago to a pleasant house on the outskirts of Fettlebridge and is an active member of the local council, and, what is more awkward, worked hard for Ember at the election. Ember reads this letter carefully: *Fettlebridge as it has existed for hundreds of years would be ruined—influx of people not used to country or small-town life—good agricultural land sterilised—traffic difficulties: poor roads, railway line already closed—duty to preserve our diminishing countryside—what do the people really want?* And so on. Ember begins to draft a suitable reply to send to the Editor of the paper, and also resolves to dictate a personal note to the Councillor suggesting that they meet to discuss the matter next week-end.

Ember is a member of Standing Committee A, which this morning is meeting at 10.30 to discuss clause 2 of the House Purchase (Temporary Provisions) Bill. Ember gathers up his constituency correspondence and goes down to the Committee Room at about 11 o'clock, looks in, and in a whisper asks the Whip if he is needed this morning. He is relieved to hear that no divisions are expected and that he needn't stay. As Ember looks around he hears his party spokesman arguing about interest rates, and he sees the Parliamentary Secretary in charge of the Bill conferring in undertones with his advisers; he turns away, goes down in the lift and crosses Old Palace Yard to meet his (half!) secretary.

Together they start to go through the constituency letters. One is unusually bulky—a petition from (as it is headed) The Parents of Fettlebridge. Ember can guess the contents: he has already been in correspondence with a number of parents over the issue of school provision for the expanded town. The Local Education Authority has proposed a system of fairly small primary schools with two comprehensive schools for the secondary stage, the post-war buildings of the existing secondary modern school to form the basis for a new technical college. Fettlebridge has no grammar school, but a number of children go to grammar schools in another town ten miles away. The petition demands grammar school provision within the expanded town. Ember has already discussed this matter at length with the chairman of his party's Education Committee and he dictates a reply in terms which echo his previous correspondence on the subject: *This is a matter for the Local Education Authority; ministerial policy in favour of comprehensive education is well known and although he is opposed to it in many respects he feels that new communities are a special case. Grammar school education will be provided within the comprehensive school. The L.E.A. scheme is a workable one. They will have ahead of them in Fettlebridge a great task in building a happy and integrated community, and the sharing of all types of children in the educational process can be a decisive influence. He doubts if a petition to Parliament will really be useful, and suggests that he arrange a meeting of the parents and members of the County Education Committee and its chief officer with himself in the chair.*

The other letters are more individual. One is an invitation to speak in his home town ('ten minutes only!' it says) at the showing of an Oxfam film. Ember will be in London that day, but he replies that he knows his wife will be delighted to speak and that he will ask her to contact his correspondent.

Most of the other letters raise personal problems. One is from a council-house tenant who needs a larger home, another from a private tenant whose landlord refuses to carry out repairs to the roof. Ember wishes that council tenants would realise that he can't dictate to the officials in the Town Hall or somehow magically get a name to the top of the housing list. However, there seems to be a case here (the tenant has a two-bedroomed flat and has just had a third baby), so Ember tells his secretary to make a copy of the letter and send it to the council's Housing Manager with a covering note. At the same time he dictates a reply to his correspondent suggesting a meeting at the 'surgery' he holds in the party committee rooms in his constituency every alternate Friday evening. Ember is unsure about the legal position of the private tenant with the unco-operative landlord. He pockets this letter intending to look up the legal points in the Library. This, he feels, is another case where it would be as well to meet the person concerned at his 'surgery'.

A long letter denounces the war in Vietnam and demands that Ember vote against the Defence Estimates. Ember sighs, and dictates a reasoned reply which takes up a valuable quarter of an hour. He doesn't expect to convince his correspondent and doubts if the writer expected to convince him either.

A letter from a retired civil servant sets out with a meticulous wealth of detail the decline in the real value of his pension. He must have missed the announcement in the House three days before that public service pensions are to be increased. Ember asks his secretary to get the relevant *Hansard* and send it off with a short note. Another letter is concerned with the writer's entitlement to industrial injury benefit: it sets out all the facts carefully and makes a convincing case; Ember suspects that the correspondent's trade union may have helped in the drafting. He asks his secretary to take a copy of the letter and send it on to the Minister of Social Security, together was a request for investigation. There must already be quite a bulky file at the local insurance office. He dictates a stereotyped reply to his constituent, saying that he has asked the Minister to look into the matter and that he will pass on the result. If the Minister's reply should be unsatisfactory, Ember will have to go over the case with the individual concerned and perhaps pursue it further by means of Parliamentary Questions, or, if the decision can be challenged, in an Adjournment Debate.

By the time he has dealt with a number of other letters, it is 12.30, and Ember walks across to the Central Lobby. He has arranged to meet for lunch two officers of his local party association who are in London for the day. At lunch in the Strangers' Dining Room, looking out over the Thames, they give Ember an account of the previous week's local elections, where some wards returned disappointing results. Conversation ranges freely over the always absorbing topic of electoral prospects. Ember brings up the subject of Fettlebridge and points out that the expansion scheme would eventually mean that constituency boundaries would have to be redrawn, with all the electoral uncertainty that that involved. His guests give an assessment of the attitude towards the scheme within the local party. They believe that opponents are now a fairly small minority. At about 2.15 they all return to the Central Lobby to watch the Speaker's procession pass on its way into the House to open the day's proceedings. Ember's guests go up to the Strangers' Gallery, for which he has given them tickets, and Ember himself walks through the Members' Lobby into the House just as Prayers are finished, and goes to his usual place on the back row of green benches on the Opposition side.

The Home Secretary is answering Questions this afternoon and Ember put down a Question some weeks before. As it stands on the Order Paper it reads:

7. Mr Ember (Dorset, East): To ask the Secretary of State for the Home Department what is the policy of the Government regarding the making of some change in the variable dates of Easter.

This subject has a long parliamentary history, and Ember has been encouraged to take it up by the holiday trade in his constituency. When the Speaker calls 'Mr Ember' he rises in his place and says 'Number 7, Sir.' The Joint Under-Secretary of State for the Home Department gets up at the despatch box, opens his folder of Answers, and reads out: 'We are awaiting the outcome of the consideration being given to this question by the World Council of Churches.' Ember is prepared for this reply and he rises again, is called by Mr Speaker, and asks his Supplementary: 'Is the Joint Under-Secretary aware that it is 39 years since the Easter Act, 1928, was passed allowing for the fixing of the date of Easter? Cannot we get agreement with the churches? Failing that, cannot we go ahead on our own and fix our own Easter?'

The Minister has envisaged a come-back on these lines and does not need to glance at his notes as he replies: 'The churches in this country, both Protestant and Roman Catholic, are agreed on the question of a fixed date, but it would be highly undesirable if the festival of Easter was on a different date in this country from that operating in the rest of the world.' Ember does not rise again and there is a rustle of Order Papers as the Speaker calls the next Member to ask Question No. 8. A fellow-Member leans towards Ember and mutters, 'Try again in five years' time.'

Ember sits on through Questions—they are concerned with the usual Home Office mixed bag of Commonwealth Immigration, crimes of violence, the prison conditions of the train robbers, police manpower, prevention of drug addiction, conditions in Borstals, reform of the law on abortion, and inflammable baby-clothes. He has heard in the Lobby that the Minister of Technology is to make a statement on the future of the Atomic Energy Authority's works at Bilslade, in a neighbouring constituency. The statement announces a new programme of work for the factory—which rumour had suggested was to be closed down—and Ember does not attempt to join in the questioning of the Minister which follows. After this, the Orders of the Day are reached. As it is a Supply Day the Opposition has the right to choose the subject for debate and they have selected the recently announced Government plans for the reorganisation and contraction of the Territorial Army. Ember does not intend to try to 'catch the Speaker's eye' and contribute to the debate, but as a 'three-line whip' has been circulated he will be required to vote at the end of the debate at 10 p.m.

As the leader of his party begins to deploy his case against the Government, Ember makes his way out of the Chamber as unobtrusively as he can, turning at the bar to bow towards the Speaker.

On his way to the cloakroom Ember glances at his watch: 3.45. He is due at a meeting of a committee of the British Timber Trades Federation at four o'clock. Parking will be difficult if he goes by car, so he walks through the subway to the Underground station and arrives at the meeting slightly breathless five minutes late. He is glad to find that cups of tea are being handed round.

The business before the committee is a draft report produced in conjunction with the Timber Development Association on the use of timber in industrialised housing. This is not, it has been decided, a suitable matter for Parliamentary Questions, still less for debate, and the report is intended for submission to the technical staff of the Ministry of Public Buildings and Works, with copies to the Ministry of Housing, the Building Research Station, a number of other interested bodies and all the firms known to be involved in industrialised building. The Federation is worried lest the new techniques should involve a diminished use of wood in house construction and has produced designs for internal non-load-bearing wall units which could be fabricated in factories and easily erected on site. After the meeting Ember stays on to talk with a fellow-member of the Federation about the effects of the Forestry Commission's increasing supplies of mature timber on the importing trade. They agree that the Federation should organise a small delegation of importers and merchants to meet the Commission and urge the marketing of this timber through normal trade channels.

It is approaching 6 o'clock when Ember returns to the House and, after signing his letters, his next engagement is a meeting of the whole parliamentary party on Defence. This is largely devoted to our 'East of Suez' commitments, and a number of speakers attack a speech made in the House the week before by a member of the 'Shadow Cabinet'. Ember speaks for a few minutes, urging that any appearance of dis-unity within the party on such an issue could have disastrous consequences. He suggests that the Shadow Cabinet should produce a statement which they can all accept and abide by.

On his way to the Smoking Room for a drink before dinner, Ember has a conversation with a Lobby correspon-dent who already seems to have a fairly good idea of what has been said at the meeting. Ember glances at the evening papers in the Smoking Room and then has dinner with two fellow back-benchers in the Members' Dining Room. One of them has been lucky in the ballot for Private Members' Bills and he manages to persuade Ember to attend the House on Fri-day to vote for the closure, which will probably be necessary as it is believed that the Government side will try to talk the Bill out.

After dinner, he makes his way to the Table Office and puts down his Question on children in hospital for the next day the Minister of Health is due to answer Questions. He goes along to the Library and looks up the point of landlord-and-tenant law his correspondent of this morning has raised, and jots down a request for the Library's Research Division to send him a note on Forestry Commission sales of various categories of timber over the last five years, and on the availability of any future projections.

As he is doing this he is approached by a back-bencher on the Government side, asking him to sign a motion which will be printed on the Order Paper the next day. The motion already has sponsors from all three parties and reads as follows:

ACCOMMODATION OF THE LEGISLATURE: That a Joint Committee of the Lords and Commons be set up to make a fundamental and comprehensive examination of the potential requirements in terms of accommodation of a modern legislature in the light of developments and changes which may occur over the course of the next half-century and of the capability of the Palace of Westminster, with such alterations and improvements as may be possible, of meeting those requirements, and to report.

Ember signs his name and then moves to an armchair and roughs out the weekly article he contributes to his local newspaper.

By this time it is 9.15; Ember returns to the Chamber to hear the two closing speeches in the debate on the Territorial Army, and afterwards records his vote with his party. The next business before the House is a Prayer to annul the Agricultural Lime Subsidy Regulations. Ember expects this will run for about an hour, and he returns to the Library to wait for the Adjournment Debate—the half-hour debate at the end of the parliamentary day. The debate is to be opened by a Government back-bencher who sits for a constituency bordering Ember's. The subject is the improvement of a trunk road which ends at Seaport in Ember's constituency, and the Member initiating the debate has promised to allow Ember five minutes for a short speech.

At 11.15 Ember hears the tape machine, which records the progress of business in the House all over the Palace, begin the clatter which signals a new announcement and as soon as he sees the 'ADJ' of 'ADJOURNMENT' appear he hurries into the Chamber. A few Members who have been discussing the previous motion are leaving, and soon the Chamber is deserted except for the Deputy Speaker in the Chair, a Clerk at the Table, the Serjeant-at-Arms, the Member speaking, Ember himself, a Government Whip and the Parliamentary Secretary to the Ministry of Transport who is to reply to the debate. Before going to his place, Ember whispers to the Deputy Speaker that the opener of the debate has agreed that he should have five minutes; he receives a nod in reply.

The government back-bencher develops his case for a high priority to be given to the improvement of the A346 and quotes a number of telling statistics of accidents, vehicle flow, population changes in the area, etc. When he sits down Ember gets to his feet and is called by the Chair. He compliments the hon. Member opposite for the skill with which he has developed his case, refers to the fact that it has the full backing of the local planning, highway and police authorities, briefly outlines its importance to Seaport—*not just a seaside resort, but also a manufacturing town and a port, making a small but important and growing contribution to our trade with Europe which will increase considerably should Britain join the Common Market*—and mentions finally the proposed expansion of Fettlebridge, which would also use the A346 as its main link with London.

When Ember sits down (he notes that he has spoken for precisely 4¾ minutes), the Parliamentary Secretary rises to reply. Ember thinks as he listens to the flow of words that this brief must be used several times a session, with just the place-names altered to suit the particular case. The Minister is saying *how glad he is to have an opportunity of discussing this important area—pays tribute to the persuasive case presented by his hon. Friend, and ably supported by the hon. Member opposite—the importance of the A346 is fully recognised by the Ministry and a number of minor improvements have been carried out since the war. However, the Ministry well recognise that more than this is needed and there is a plan for extensive stretches of dual carriageway . . .* here the Government back-bencher interjects 'That plan was made 14 years ago'—*but he is sorry to say that he can give no firm starting date for actual road works. It is unfortunately his duty to consider a large number of demands—all of them, no doubt, of the greatest local importance—and this particu-*

lar scheme—valuable though it would be—has to take its place in the queue.

The Parliamentary Secretary is a practised speaker in Adjournment Debates and his rounded close comes almost on the dot 30 minutes after the debate began. Immediately he sits down, the Deputy Speaker rises, the Serjeant removes the mace, and the House is adjourned for the day.

Ember walks across the floor to the bench on the Government side of the House where his fellow-fighter for the improvement of the A346 is gathering up his notes. They smile ruefully and walk out of the Chamber together towards the Smoking Room for a night-cap. They are joined in a few minutes by the Parliamentary Secretary.

'We shall have to get you people out', says Ember with a smile.

'You could have your road tomorrow if you'd vote for another shilling on the income tax', replies the Parliamentary Secretary. 'You should see the list of schemes all ready to go, bar the money. So long as you don't use it in evidence against me, I can tell you that your road is about six years away.'

'Never mind,' says the Government back-bencher to Ember, 'you may be in his shoes before then.'

'You still wouldn't be able to fish it out of the queue', says the Parliamentary Secretary with a grim smile.

* * *

At the end of the day we have described Ember was in bed half an hour after midnight and fell asleep over the White Paper on the Adult Offender which had been issued that afternoon. As he dozed off he reminded himself to telephone his wife in the morning.

8

Another Place

'WE THE Lords Spiritual and Temporal, welcome this occasion of commemorating and celebrating with Your Majesty and with Members of the House of Commons the seven hundredth anniversary of the Parliament to which were summoned for the first time to our certain knowledge the Citizens and Burgesses, as well as the Knights of the Shire, *to join with the Lords in deliberation upon the needs and affairs of the Realm.* The Parliament summoned to meet in January 1265 by Your Majesty's forebear, King Henry the Third, at the instance of Simon de Montfort, Earl of Leicester, thus contained *all the essential elements of later Parliaments*'*.

The words of the Lord Chancellor in Westminster Hall in June 1965 remind us that, apart from a short break in the mid-seventeenth century, the House of Lords has always been an integral part of Parliament. Lords and Commons meet separately at Westminster, and they are constituted on very different principles; but the process of legislation concerns them both. In Parliament to-day, the House of Commons predominates; but despite long-standing proposals to abolish or radically reform the House of Lords, this non-elected, largely hereditary Second Chamber survives. And no account of the British Parliament is complete without a brief mention of the body which Members of the House of Commons often refer to as 'another place'.

Of all Second Chambers, the House of Lords remains to this day the most numerous and the most hereditary; it has changed less as regards its constitution than any other legislative body with a life-span even remotely approaching its own.

* Authors' italics.

How is it that such an assembly has survived within the context of a democratic system? The answer may be found partly in the course of British history and partly in the widespread use which is made of 'Second Chambers', or 'Upper Houses', in contemporary legislatures abroad. Even Russia, which has little place for tradition and no place for parliamentary government, has a Supreme Soviet consisting of two Chambers: the Soviet of the Union and the Soviet of Nationalities.

In her study of *English Constitutional Theory and the House of Lords* from 1556 to 1832, Dr Corinne Weston points out that an important reason why so few political reformers criticised the role of the House of Lords in Britain before 1832 was the general acceptance of the so-called classical constitutional theory of 'mixed' government. From Tudor times, it was widely held that the English system of government successfully combined the three simple or 'unmixed' types—monarchy, aristocracy and democracy, avoiding by the inherent checks and balances of such a mixture the individual weaknesses and vices of the three pure forms of government. The place of the House of Lords within such a composite framework was clear and unquestioned. Ironically it was King Charles I who made one of the most specific and outspoken defences of this division of political power. In his *Answer to the XIX Propositions of both Houses of Parliament*, printed and circulated in 1642, he declared:

> There being three kinds of Government amongst men, Absolute Monarchy, Aristocracy and Democracy, and all these having their particular conveniences and inconveniences. The experience and wisdom of your Ancestors hath so moulded this out of a mixture of these, as to give to this Kingdom . . . the conveniences of all three, without the inconveniences of any one, as long as the Balance hangs even between the three Estates. . . .

Theoretical pronouncements of this kind do not prove that bicameralism originated in a conscious belief that it provided the best basis for a parliamentary system. As with the British Parliament generally, so it was with the House of Lords: practice preceded and shaped doctrine. The Upper House may be said to have first become a distinct 'Second Chamber' when the elected citizens and burgesses and the knights of the shires began to meet and deliberate in their own Commons' House. Nevertheless, the view that an aristocratic Second Chamber was politically desirable, even indispensable, within the accepted framework of a 'limited' democracy grew up and prevailed until well after the Reform Act of 1832. Its cause was helped by the absence of any fundamental frictions between the two Chambers themselves.

Members of the Commons, many of whom were wealthy upper-class men, shared a great deal of the political interests and aspirations of the House of Lords. Quite often they owed their nomination to the active constituency support of individual peers. In addition, the established and clear-cut class structure of English society both promoted and sustained the continuing vitality and power of the Lords. Constitutional considerations apart, it was widely felt that the hereditary rights of the Upper House were justly enjoyed by virtue of the supposedly superior breeding and talents of its members.

The Reform Act of 1832 did not at once disturb this balance of power. Both Whigs and Tories at that time were anxious not to convert the system of mixed government into what might be termed a pure democracy, where political power was wholly concentrated in the House of Commons. Nevertheless, in the eventful years which followed, a social and political gulf between the hereditary Chamber and its elected partner in Parliament gradually established itself. Already in June 1833 Macaulay had described (in a letter to his sister) his reactions to a formal conference of both Houses in a manner which anticipated future developments:

The Lords sat in little cocked hats along a table; and we stood uncovered at the other side and delivered in our resolutions. I thought that before long it may be our turn to sit, and theirs to stand.

Twenty-six years later Sir James Graham was prompted to remark that the days when a conclave of Dukes could sway a Parliament had vanished.* The widening franchise, the growing influence of the industrial middle classes and the general upsurge of democratic ideas combined to make the *status quo* eventually untenable, as far as the House of Lords was concerned; and in 1909, Mr Lloyd George proclaimed in unequivocal terms the injustice of a bicameral system which allowed 500 'ordinary men chosen accidentally from among the unemployed' to defeat the wishes of the millions of people engaged 'in the industry which makes the wealth of the country'.

Despite such fighting words, and notwithstanding the Parliament Acts of 1911 and 1949, the House of Lords remains. Its wings have been severely clipped, of course. But it can still make its presence felt. As the House of Commons claimed and won greater powers for itself, as Britain moved towards a more effectively democratic method of parliamentary government, so at the same time the more conservative element amongst the people themselves came to regard the House of Lords as a very necessary curb on the potential dangers of a supreme and aggressive elected Chamber. This unexpected development harks back to the centuries-old doctrine of mixed government. Its strength reposes as much on vague, unspoken fears of mass-rule and on an emotional respect for the past as much as it does on reasoned political argument: but its modern importance as a conserving influence is beyond doubt. Surprisingly, but incontrovertibly, some honest and respected citizens of to-day regard the preservation of a largely hereditary House of Lords as being just as important as the survival of parliamentary democracy.

But the course of British history, coupled with the mystique of hereditary rank, cannot be held solely responsible for

* *Life of Sir James Graham*, II, p. 366 (cited by Sir Ivor Jennings in *Cabinet Government*, 3rd edn., p. 490).

the international popularity of the bicameral parliamentary system. That popularity is considerable. In the United States of America, national legislative power is vested in a Congress composed of a Senate and a House of Representatives. The former contains two members from each state, each of whom is elected by popular vote for a period of six years; every other year, one-third of the members retire or seek re-election. The House of Representatives consists of 435 members, the number from each state being determined in proportion to the latest census of population.

Amongst the American *state* legislatures, moreover, Nebraska alone has a single Chamber: the remainder are all bicameral. The Norwegian Parliament, or Storting, splits up into two Chambers; the Lagting consists of a quarter of the members of the whole Parliament (by whom they are chosen) while the remaining 112 members compose the Odelsting. And so on around the world: Peru has its Senate and Chamber of Deputies; Australia's Federal Parliament and all its state legislatures, with the exception (since 1922) of Queensland, have two Chambers. The Shura (Parliament) in Afghanistan consists of the directly elected House of the People—or Wolesi Jirgah—and the House of Elders, or Mesrano Jirgah, one-third of whose members are appointed by the King for a five-year period. Ireland has its Seanad and its Dail.

Why do so many countries, not one of which subscribes to the hereditary principle of the British Second Chamber,* divide their legislature into two distinct assemblies? Some of them, such as the United States and Switzerland, operate a federal system of government and thus have a special reason for wishing to maintain two Chambers. The lower House is numerically representative of the whole population; the upper House provides for the equal representation of their

---

* A few countries, for example Sweden and the Netherlands, call their popular directly elected body the 'Second Chamber'. But the majority of countries use the term in the opposite sense, and this practice has been adopted in the present chapter.

states and cantons. But the general underlying and functional motive almost everywhere is the desire to have a 'second opinion' when it comes to deciding matters of national importance. George Washington spoke of the 'senatorial saucer' into which legislation, hot from the popular assembly, could be poured in order to cool. J. S. Mill similarly warned of the dangers of having a single, despotic legislative body 'released from the necessity of considering whether its acts will be concurred in by another constituted authority'.

The value of making provision for the expression of second thoughts within any legislature is twofold—in theory, if not always in practice. It affords a delaying opportunity, that is to say it offers more time for controversial legislation to be considered and for imperfectly drafted Bills to be improved. It also subjects matters of public concern to the scrutiny of a different kind of assembly whose members are not exposed in the same degree to the thoroughly proper but distracting pressures which are brought to bear on the directly elected popular assembly. These 'revising' functions lie at the heart of the modern role and importance of Second Chambers.

Following the advent of strong party organisation, however, it must be conceded that practice does not always coincide with doctrine in the above respect. If the party struggle is to be carried into the Second Chamber, then the latter may simply approve the decisions of its legislative partner when the political complexion of both Houses is the same; but when the political make-up is different, it will tend to block the will of the representative assembly. In the one instance, the Second Chamber would be superfluous, while in the other it could be mischievous. One way of avoiding such a dilemma concerns the composition of the non-elected body, and is discussed later. But there is another and simpler remedy, already adopted by many countries, and that is to ensure that the Second Chamber is less powerful than its partner. Thus the British House of Lords is viewed to-day as a 'useful' rather than as a 'strong' body. Sides were still being taken on this issue in the thirties, but there exists widespread agreement to-day that the two Chambers must not function as rivals. They are partners—but the success of the partnership depends on the inequality of the two bodies.

This imbalance does not of itself guarantee that the peers of the British realm are powerless to hinder the legislative intentions of the Commons. A Bill sent up late in the session could conceivably be thrown out (if it is not a Money Bill) and might not find another place for itself, in view of habitually crowded timetables, for many years to come. The fact that relatively few serious confrontations of this sort come about is due partly to the tacitly acknowledged primacy of the one assembly over the other and partly to the exercise of common sense all round. In 1965, for example, the House of Lords proposed certain amendments to the Labour Government's War Damage Bill which, had they been incorporated, would have radically altered the effect and scope of the legislation. The Commons rejected the Lords' amendments and the latter, in consequence, were faced with a critical decision. Should they insist on their point of view? On May 25, 1965, the Marquess of Salisbury summed up the situation thus:

> I rise . . . to urge your Lordships, with all diffidence, not to insist further on our Amendments. If I do this, I can assure your Lordships that it is not because I do not realise the importance of the issues raised by the War Damage Bill, especially in respect of the retrospective element contained in it. That is why people like myself (and I suppose that I am typical of many other noble Lords, at any rate on this side of the House) were in favour of inserting these Amendments on the Committee stage of the Bill—and, my Lords, I still think we were quite right. It was, I believe, not only justifiable but desirable that we should give Members of another place another chance of looking at, and discussing, the issues raised, in the light of views expressed by eminent lawyers and others in your Lordships' House.
>
> But, my Lords, the position now is quite different, and is far more formidable than it was at that time. For if we insist further, we shall, in my view . . . be provoking a first-class

crisis between the two Houses of Parliament; and that, after all, is no light matter.

The status and function of a twentieth-century Second Chamber could scarcely have been better expressed. And having made their point, the Lords yielded to the wishes of the Commons.

In Britain and certain other parliamentary régimes the Cabinet system of government also favours the subordination of the one Chamber to the other. The Government is in Parliament: the Prime Minister and his Cabinet colleagues therefore need the majority support of Parliament. Whenever serious disagreement arises between the two Chambers, the Cabinet can properly be responsible to only one of them, and quite clearly the will of the elected body must prevail. If in Britain a Labour Government were called upon to answer for its actions not only to the House of Commons, where the majority favoured its policies, but also to an equally powerful House of Lords with a built-in Conservative majority, then parliamentary government would grind to a halt.

The dangers and frustrations of such a situation were certainly in Mr Harold Wilson's mind when, in a speech at Blackpool in March 1965, he warned the House of Lords that if they decided to obstruct the Government's programme the Labour Party would seek a mandate at the next General Election 'to amend the Parliament Act so as to end the Lords' power to block Commons' legislation'. One year later, the Labour Party's Election Manifesto announced that 'legislation will be introduced to safeguard measures approved by the House of Commons from frustration by delay or defeat in the House of Lords'. Already in 1918, however, the general point had been made by Viscount Bryce in his report to the then Prime Minister* on the Second Chamber Conference set up the previous year. A Second Chamber, he said, ought not to have equal powers with the House of Commons:

* Rt. Hon. David Lloyd George. See Cd. [Command Paper] 9038 of 1918

In particular it should not have the power of making or unmaking Ministries, or enjoy equal rights in dealing with finance. This was prescribed not only by long-established custom and tradition, but also by the form of our Constitution, which makes the Executive depend upon the support of the House of Commons, and would be seriously affected in its working by extending to a Second Chamber the power of dismissing a Government.

The role of the House of Lords as a subordinate partner to the elected Chamber is now firmly established and generally accepted, and the late Lord Pethick-Lawrence, in a debate on House of Lords Reform in October 1957* described the Second Chamber as an anomaly which, on the whole, worked extremely well. But maximum usefulness, according to a good many critics, is only possible if the House of Lords is also a different *kind* of assembly from the Commons, if its members are able to offer an independent and a fresh set of opinions on many of the important matters coming before Parliament. And the simple distinction afforded by the hereditary basis of the British Second Chamber is held by such critics to be insufficient for this purpose. Viscount Samuel, in the same debate of October 1957, expressed this point of view most forcibly:

> Parties are necessary in a democracy, to organise and to give stability both to the electorate and to the Legislature. But when the party system goes so far as to crush our independent minds, then it does enormous mischief, and it is quite certain that under our present régime . . . there has been a considerable crushing of the independent mind. There is no doubt that in the nation at large, in all classes and in all parts of the country, there are men and women who might be of the greatest value to the community, but who have not the time or the temperament or the willingness to face the turmoil, the strains and the preoccupations of strenuous Parliamentary life. . . . We should . . . take steps to recruit [them] and, indeed, to a great extent, change the character of your Lordships' House, which might play an immense part in giving leader-

* October 30 and 31, 1957.

ship to the nation and to public opinion, not only in matters of politics but in all the great questions that vex the public mind.

A legislative assembly which is divorced from party politics is of course an impossibility, and it is clear that the party struggle must always, to a limited extent at least, be reflected in both Chambers. Viscount Samuel's speech, however, challenged the essentially hereditary, and therefore nowadays largely unrepresentative, basis of the House of Lords on the grounds that it allowed too few opportunities for men and women *of all classes and of no particular party* to play their part in parliamentary life. Taken to its logical conclusion, this sort of argument anticipates the possible future role of the British Second Chamber both as an antidote to the strangle-hold of party discipline in Parliament, and as a means of strengthening and broadening the base of parliamentary criticism and scrutiny of the Executive. A consequence would be that the status and the influence, if not the legislative power, of the Lords would be enhanced. And although the Second Chamber might never be a directly elected assembly, it would be a more representative body in that its members would reflect more accurately the realities of public life.

The Conservative Government's Life Peerage Act came into force in April 1958. Its gift to the constitution of non-hereditary peerages was received with mixed feelings, both inside and outside Parliament. The late Hugh Gaitskell voiced serious doubts, during the Second Reading debate, as to its intentions.

> Why, and for what purpose, is it desirable to enhance the prestige of the House of Lords? Can it have any other significance except to increase its authority? The right hon. Gentleman must pardon us if we [the Labour Party] believe that this is what lies behind the mind of the Government. We have had a good deal of trouble over a long period of time with the House of Lords. We know that there are proposals for reform being bandied about . . . and we know that the main

motive behind these proposals is to preserve the authority and enhance the prestige of the House of Lords.

It would be unrealistic to claim that even to-day the hoped-for tonic effect of a steady trickle of life peers into the Lords has made a fundamental impact either on that assembly itself or on public opinion concerning its usefulness. But it has allowed a number of distinguished men and women from different walks of life to contribute to the work of Parliament, and inevitably the influence and authority of such people will increase. A report in the *Sunday Telegraph* of January 23, 1966, headed 'Room at the Top for Eminent Independents', observed that the allocation of a room 'carved out of Westminster's cramped accommodation' to the 80 or so Independent peers marked the

> ... growing importance of a group whose mentors are Lord Strang, former Permanent Head of the Foreign Office, Baroness Swanborough, widow of the first Lord Reading and founder of the W.V.S. and Lord Iddesleigh, Roman Catholic grandson of the statesman who, in 1887, dropped dead while visiting Lord Salisbury at No. 10 Downing Street.
>
> As their title implies, they are not a party and have no leader. But they take new peers under their wings and have prepared notes on the customs of the Upper House for the guidance of fledglings.

Since, moreover, a relatively small number of peers play an active role in the day-to-day business of the House, the importance of determined and conscientious newcomers is even greater than might at first appear. A further reform, the 1963 Peerage Act, made it possible for a 'reluctant peer' to renounce his hereditary title for life. Mr Wedgwood Benn lost no time in executing his instrument of disclaimer, and he was soon followed by others. The long-term effect of the Peerage Act on the status of the House of Lords itself is at present not clear. But, contrary to logical expectations, it could result in increased influence for the Second Chamber as the latter became more and more a place for men and women 'who have got there on merit'.*

But when all has been said, the present composition of the House of Lords is still far removed from the stated intention of the Asquith Government—in the preamble to the Parliament Act of 1911—to arrive at a Second Chamber constituted on a popular basis. There are of course familiar explanations of the very modest dilution of the hereditary principle achieved to date. Diversity of counsel is certainly one reason: we have noted the perfectly legitimate desire of some people to preserve the hereditary basis as an alleged curb on the potential dangers of 'mass rule' and of an 'arrogantly independent' unicameral legislature. Another conserving influence is the cautious, pragmatic, traditionally-minded temperament of the British people, who have generally preferred to advance one step at a time rather than risk a giant's stride into the unknown.

Most important of all, there is no gainsaying the substantial and valuable contributions of the present House of Lords to the work of Parliament. In some respects, the Second Chamber may be said to have been more progressive, and certainly less sensitive to public opinion, than the Commons in the post-war years—for example, on controversial issues such as abortion and homosexuality. And in the context of modern parliamentary life, where the Commons are grappling desperately with the problem of an overcrowded timetable, the detailed scrutiny of legislation which the Second Chamber is able and willing to undertake has proved invaluable. But the result of all these factors has been that the crucial problem of the composition of the Lords remains largely unresolved. Should we continue to tinker with the ermine, or should both the advantages and the risks of a radical overhaul be squarely faced? Here is an issue which must appeal to the stoutest of hearts.

* V. Weare, 'The House of Lords—Prophecy and Fulfilment', in *Parliamentary Affairs*, Autumn 1965, p. 427.

Second Chambers are not essential to the working of modern parliamentary government. At first sight they may even appear to be a complicating factor which can only confuse the process of democratic scrutiny and control of the Executive. This is one reason why some of the younger countries which subscribe to the parliamentary system have dispensed altogether with the idea of a bicameral legislature, preferring instead to have a direct and simple confrontation between the elected representatives of the people on the one hand, and the Government on the other. Grave doubts as to the usefulness of the Senate in Kenya—one of the few new African states which chose to have two Chambers instead of one—have existed for three years,* and J. H. Proctor, Jr., recently concluded an article in *Parliamentary Affairs* (Autumn 1965, p. 415) as follows:

> Although given a new lease of life, it remains on probation. Whether Kenya can afford to maintain an institution which actually contributes no more than has the Senate may well become increasingly doubtful. If, however, in attempting to accomplish more, it seems to be obstructing the Government, it may well be swept quickly away. The challenge facing the Senate of Kenya at present is to discover ways of participating in the governing process that will justify but not jeopardise its existence.

In long-established régimes where Second Chambers have been an integral part of the legislature from the start, where they have proved their usefulness and evinced some willingness to adapt themselves to modern democratic principles, the question of doing away with them in the interests of simplicity does not arise to any serious extent. They are envisaged as a useful, if not indispensable, component of Parliament. But it is very necessary nevertheless to see their contemporary role in a clear perspective. Thus the early function of an aristocratic House of Lords in a 'mixed' constitution—to

* Under the terms of a Parliamentary Constituencies Review Order, published on October 19, 1966, it was announced that the Senate would be dissolved.

curb the popular will—has largely disappeared. Its modern purpose, by majority consent, is to help and not to hinder the Commons; and there are many people to-day who would like to see its composition reviewed and its status enhanced in order that its role be more sharply defined, and its participation expanded, in the processes of modern democratic—and representative—government.

Further Reading

P. A. Bromhead: *The House of Lords and Contemporary Politics, 1911–1957*, Routledge, 1958.

9
Westminster and the World

As with the concept of democracy, so it is with the institution of Parliament: few countries to-day are unwilling to pay tribute to the value and importance of a representative assembly or congress, elected by the people and occupying a high position within the constitution. But these tributes are, in too many instances, lip-service only. The perils of a purely symbolic, non-effective Parliament have already been mentioned, and there is no need to rehearse here the various ways in which the semblance of democracy can be exploited to serve the purposes of totalitarian government. But the point is worth making, if only in passing, that representative government must correspond to a fundamental, even emotional need or aspiration of peoples the world over, since so many basically undemocratic, non-parliamentary régimes are anxious to appear the contrary of what they are. And this phenomenon is an indirect illustration, at least, of the influence of the oldest of living Parliaments in the world at large.

The political axiom that almost all the world's genuine legislative assemblies were either imitated directly from, or inspired by, the British model survived the World War of 1939–45 and found its modern practical expression in those Westminster-type constitutions handed on to former colonial territories when they became independent. When John Bright uttered his now too-famous words over a century ago, that England was the Mother of Parliaments, few of his contemporaries at home or abroad were disposed to quarrel with his claim. But in the last ten years or so, serious doubts have been raised as to whether more or less faithful copies of the British Parliament are in fact the best answer to the constitutional and political dilemmas of many other countries—particularly those of the emerging states of Africa.

Fears and criticisms of this sort imply an acceptance of the direct influence of Westminster but question the effectiveness of that influence. As Hill and Whichelow put it (in their study *What's Wrong with Parliament?*): 'Ours may be the Mother of Parliaments, but not all her children can fill her with pride; at their best, some of them are only good in parts'. Before we turn to this aspect of comparative parliamentary studies, however, it may be interesting and instructive to consider the general historical validity of Bright's claim.

The old Spanish Cortes (or parliaments)—composed of bishops, noblemen and burgesses—antedated Simon de Montfort's famous English Parliament of 1265 by about a hundred years, and are therefore probably the earliest known example of attempts at parliamentary government. (Before that, the Icelandic Althing, or common court, had been established for certain legislative and judicial purposes.) But England's is the Parliament with the longest line of unbroken development, and fully deserves the title of 'Mother of Parliaments' in the straightforward historical sense of the phrase. It had been developing for hundreds of years, testing and improving itself (often unwittingly) against the background of domestic history, before most countries had even thought of setting up a similar form of national government.

The spontaneous creation of free institutions has always proved to be a precarious, if not totally impossible, undertaking; nothing was more natural, therefore, than that both political theorists and practising statesmen of the eighteenth century should seek to benefit from the accumulated experience and wisdom of the single established model. When delegates, themselves of British descent, met at Philadelphia in 1787 to devise a form of American central government, they were certainly strongly influenced by their knowledge and assessment of the Parliament at Westminster. And when

Alexander Hamilton wrote, in his *Federalist*, that the science of politics 'has received great improvement' and that 'the efficacy of various principles is now well understood, which were either not known at all, or imperfectly known to the Ancients', we may be sure that his various principles were based partly at least on British practice.

But the American so-called 'copy' of the British legislature was soon to develop important differences from the Parliament of the mother country. Admittedly those early political scientists believed that they were less opposed to the British model than they actually were when they stipulated that there should be a clear constitutional separation between the legislative and executive bodies, between Congress and the President. At that time, the Cabinet system, the vital link between Government and Parliament at Westminster, was neither fully developed nor properly understood; and the doctrine of the separation of powers, attributed (not altogether correctly) to Montesquieu's assessment of the British constitution, was not considered to be incompatible with imitation of the latter. But this deliberate severance of the Executive from the legislative assembly has never been seriously questioned since its inception in the United States, and it differs so crucially from British constitutional practice to-day that we must now distinguish between 'presidential' and 'parliamentary' systems of representative government.

It may be argued that this classic distinction between the American system and our own should not be held against England's claim to be the Mother of *Parliaments*, as opposed to the legislatures existing under a presidential régime. But a study of the Cabinet system in certain countries which subscribe to parliamentary government reveals important differences in principle and practice between those states and the British 'model'. In Britain the Prime Minister and his Cabinet colleagues hold office as long as they have the effective confidence of the House of Commons; by convention, moreover, ministers are invariably members of either the

Lords or Commons. Thus, when Mr Patrick Gordon Walker★ became Foreign Secretary in October 1964, despite having lost his former seat in Parliament as MP for Smethwick, he almost immediately sought re-election in another constituency. Again unsuccessful, he resigned his ministerial post and the Member for Fulham (Mr Michael Stewart) was appointed in his stead. In many Commonwealth countries, a similar situation exists. But under certain continental parliamentary régimes ministers are explicitly debarred from being full members of the legislature.

At first sight it might appear that countries which apply this rule, like France, Holland, Luxembourg and Norway, practise the presidential system proper, including the doctrine of the separation of powers. This is not true: their ministers hold office as long as they have the confidence of their respective Parliaments. They may have been members of the legislature immediately prior to taking up office, and they may stand for re-election at the next General Election. Moreover, such ministers are permitted to sit and to speak in Parliament (sometimes in both Chambers) although they do not vote. The Government, therefore, is not strictly separated from the legislature; each is dependent on and influences the other in a much more intimate fashion than is the case in Washington. Nevertheless, major divergences between such parliamentary régimes and British practice are evident: in the former, there clearly exists a degree of independence, as opposed to complete separation, between the legislative and executive bodies which is quite foreign to Westminster.

Parliaments are national institutions and they have to function amid the different and changing political, economic and social environments of their respective countries. They each have their origin and continuing vitality in the desire of a particular nation to solve its own constitutional and political problems; and because the latter are not the same in any two countries the legislatures reveal important, far-reaching

★ Since April 1966, M.P. for Leyton.

differences both among themselves and from the British model. (It was in this sense that Rousseau wrote to Mirabeau that the whole science of government was the study of combinations, applications and exceptions—in keeping with the time, the place and circumstances.) Thus, the device of federalism is the invention of the United States of America. At Philadelphia in 1787 there were, very broadly speaking, two opposing sets of opinion, the one favouring a powerful national government and the other anxious to preserve as far as possible the powers of the separate states. The result of these conflicting ideals may be seen to-day in the working of the United States as a federal constitution: the central, or federal authority acts for certain purposes which are stated in the constitution, while in other fields the individual states abide by the decisions of their own state governments. The operation, or otherwise, of capital punishment is thus a matter for a particular state, whereas in this country the passing of Mr Sydney Silverman's Bill in November 1965 meant that nowhere in Britain could the death penalty be enforced for murder.

Federalism, moreover, has since been freely adopted in certain European, South American and Commonwealth countries—often as a means of meeting the representative requirements of a non-homogeneous population. In such countries the central federal legislature is obliged to function in a very different context from that of the British Parliament.

The role of national character and the pattern of public life are also important in the shaping of a country's institutions. For instance, Walter Bagehot wrote a series of letters to the *Inquirer* in 1852 in which he argued that Frenchmen were 'too clever' for permanent and strong 'British' parliamentary government. A contemporary Bagehot would be more inclined to point to the numerous, widespread and deep-rooted divergences in political and social beliefs, not to mention the extremes of temperament, which are still to be found so close to the surface of French public life. These fundamental differences—whether between the politically extreme right wing and the strong, articulate Communist Party, or between the sophisticated urban élites of Paris and Bordeaux and the vital, rough simplicity of the true *paysan* —do not provide that stable, broadly homogeneous background of opinion which is an important condition of parliamentary government *à l'anglaise*. (In general terms, both Fascism and Communism have been rejected in Britain because they lie outside this broad consensus of opinion.)

Not surprisingly, therefore, several modern political commentators have noted a recurring pattern of political and personal behaviour in France which militates against the enduring success of strong parliamentary government. Bagehot was referring in 1852 to the downfall of the Second Republic and to the powerful executive régime under Napoleon III which replaced it: his remarks might be applied, with some justification, to the extensive *executive* powers of the present Fifth Republic under President de Gaulle, which succeeded the Fourth Republic in 1958. During the combined lifetimes of the latter and its predecessor, the Third Republic, well over one hundred changes of Government had taken place, the legislature choosing and dismissing administrations more or less at will and providing at times an illustration of how parliamentary government in the British tradition can fail to answer the needs of a foreign country.

There are many significant similarities, as well as contrasts, between the British Parliament and the great legislatures of the world which have grown up subsequently. The two-Chamber system has its origins in the separate existence of our own Lords and Commons. But even here, the extent of the imitation has been limited; the hereditary principle, for example, has been rejected. The office of Speaker, or President, plays a vital role in the working of most elected parliamentary assemblies. There can be no doubt of England's claim to be the first in this particular field; nevertheless, individual legislatures have allotted vastly differing roles to their respective presiding officers. Thus the complete political impartiality of the Speakership which characterises the British office does not apply in Australia or New Zealand; there have been occasions in Canberra, unthinkable at Westminster, when Mr Speaker has been accused of rank political partiality and his personal character impugned in the process. The simple point to be made here is that the parliamentary practices of Australia owe as much to the robust and developing temperament of that nation as they do to the traditions of Westminster. As Philip Laundy puts it in *The Office of Speaker*: 'Theirs is a raw and unpolished democracy.... They would certainly offer short shrift to any parliamentary purist who attempted to pass pious judgments on their practices'.

Britain's claim to have established the concept of an official Leader of the Opposition is justified in a general sense, and no doubt can exist that the institution has proved to be one of the greatest political innovations of all time. But the British were not really the first to recognise, in a practical way, the importance of the office. Whereas no salary was payable to the Leader of the Opposition in the House of Commons until 1937, Canada and Australia had adopted the practice of paying such a salary well before that date. It was in 1905 in fact that the Canadian Prime Minister, proposing the payment of a sessional allowance to the Leader of the Opposition, described the office as being just as important as that of the Prime Minister.

The British *type* of national parliamentary government, although the first and the oldest, is neither the single viable model nor necessarily the best model in all respects. The tendency to regard different practices abroad as deviations from the norm is restricting and potentially harmful, yet great parliamentarians have succumbed to the temptation. Sir Winston Churchill once referred to the numerous 'semi-circular assemblies' abroad, which provided each Member with his own seat, his own desk and his own desk-lid to bang, and suggested that logical arrangements of this sort had proved fatal to parliamentary government 'as we know it here in its home and in the land of its birth'. Sir Winston was arguing the particular localised case for rebuilding the new Commons' Chamber in its traditional oblong form, and no doubt his fellow-Members in 1943 understood his indirect allusion to, *inter alia*, the semicircular Chamber of Deputies of the French Third Republic. Generally speaking, however, there is no overwhelming evidence against the practicability of the parliamentary amphitheatre; it may not suit our domestic requirements and preferences, but it has succeeded in some Commonwealth and in many foreign legislatures. Westminster is but one of several models in the context of world parliamentarianism.

Perhaps the most striking contemporary illustration of this is to be found in the European Parliament of the six Common Market countries. Whether or not it would have been closer to the Westminster model had Britain been a founder-member of EEC is an academic question which need not concern us here. The fact is that the European Parliament is much closer to the continental (and particularly to the French) type of legislature, both as regards its seating arrangements and its procedure, than it is to the British.*

Its practice of allowing oral questions certainly derives in part from the British tradition, although the Bundestag in Bonn also has this type of critical scrutiny of the Executive. But the committees of the European Parliament, unlike those at Westminster, are permanent and specialised, and their functions are clearly based on those of French parliamentary committees. Thus debates in plenary session are normally held 'on the report of the appropriate committee' (Article 29), after the latter has made the initial examination of legislative proposals. Voting, again in keeping with continental traditions, is generally by a show of hands (Article 35). And members of the Parliament sit in a hemicycle facing the dais which

* Cf., e.g., Murray Forsyth, *The Parliament of the European Communities*, P.E.P., 1964, p. 39.

is occupied by their President. In the light of such developments, many of the apparently essential attributes of the parliamentary system as it is practised at Westminster will be seen to be dispensable even though they may be highly desirable. There could still be a genuine British Parliament, for example, if both the hereditary monarchy and the House of Lords were abolished and if the present committee system were radically overhauled. It would even be possible for MPs to sit in a hemicycle and bang the lids of their own desks.

In what sense, then, is it indisputably true that England is the effective Mother (that is, model or prototype) of Parliaments? To assess Westminster's greatest contribution to the world of political theory and practice we must turn away from the details of a particular constitution (and the British constitution itself is still in process of evolution) and return to the basic idea of Parliament that the necessity of authority and the demands of liberty are capable of coming together in a relationship which can offer government by majority decision and attempt the reconciliation of opposing views by compromise and agreement. It is this fundamental verity which the long history of the British Parliament has done more to establish and illustrate than has any other national or international institution.

It is true that dissentient voices have made themselves heard even on this score. Jean-Jacques Rousseau maintained in his *Contrat Social* that although the English regarded themselves as free men under their parliamentary system they were in fact only free during the election of Members of Parliament: subsequently they were overtaken by slavery. But his great contemporary, Voltaire, thought differently and history has proved him right. During his stay in eighteenth-century London he grew convinced that 'the English are the one nation on earth who have succeeded in limiting the powers of the monarch by resisting them; and who, after a series of struggles, have at last set up that wise form of government in which the king, all-powerful to do good works, is at the same time prevented from doing harm; where the nobles are without arrogance ... where the people share in the rule of law without causing confusion'. This famous extract from Voltaire's *Letters Concerning the English Nation*, first published in 1733, is matched by another graphic description:

> Not long since Mr Shippen [a respected Tory MP] began his speech in the House of Commons with these words: 'The *majesty* of the *people* of England would be wounded'. The strangeness of the expression caused much laughter. But this gentleman, far from being discouraged, repeated the same words in a resolute tone of voice—and the laughter ceased.

More than two hundred years later, government by representative discussion and consent was still the rule at Westminster during the dark months of 1940 and 1941: Parliament was demonstrating, as never before, that it was an extremely effective instrument of government as well as a genuinely democratic institution. Bertrand de Jouvenel* has summed up very well the nature of the indebtedness of other countries to the Westminster Parliament. He was visiting an old friend at the House of Commons shortly after the end of the war: 'How thankful I felt, standing in the hall, that the institution had withstood the turmoil, and was available to the world as a much-needed tutor in the practices of political liberty!'

The second line of thought prompted by the words of John Bright concerns the suitability, or otherwise, of the Westminster model for those former British colonial territories which have received their independence in the postwar years. The current situation here is, most emphatically, neither as clear nor as hopeful as the mother country would have wished. Parliamentary government has failed in Pakistan; while many of the new African nation-states are experiencing, to say the least, serious difficulties in making the parliamentary system work. In January 1966, the Nigerian Prime Minister, Sir Abubakar Tafawa Balewa, and two

* In *Government and Opposition*, Vol. 1, No. 1, October 1965, p. 135.

regional Premiers were killed when the army seized power—in a country which, so it had been optimistically hoped, might have proved to be a showcase for Westminster-type democracy. Barely six weeks later, the Ghanaian *coup d'état* deposed the seemingly impregnable President Nkrumah. These are perhaps extreme cases: but elsewhere—in Tanzania and Uganda, for instance—there have been drastic deviations from the type of parliamentary government practised in Britain and many of the older Commonwealth countries.

On reflection, these 'deviations' are not in themselves as surprising as might as first appear. As an institutional and conceptual export, parliamentary government cannot simply be transported across the seas like a railway locomotive and planted on the shores of some newly independent country, there to fulfil its allotted purposes. History has already amply demonstrated this truism. Ironically perhaps, the thesis that England's position as the Mother of Parliaments must depend ultimately on the *general* example of representative democracy which it can still provide is being confirmed to-day in many countries which originally modelled themselves closely on the distinctively British type of government. A cursory glance at the political map of Africa illustrates this.

In May 1963, 32 independent African nations met at Addis Ababa to sign their Charter of Unity; all but a few of those states were former colonial territories, and some such as Ghana, Sierra Leone, Nigeria, Tanganyika (now Tanzania) and Uganda had been granted their independence by Britain in the post-war years. Before severing her colonial ties, Britain had tried to plant and nurture in those countries the seeds of her own brand of parliamentary government, with properly elected legislatures and a recognised Opposition as at Westminster. A former Clerk of the House of Commons, the late Sir Frederic Metcalfe, went out to Nigeria to become Speaker of the Legislative Assembly there. To-day, many of these institutions still exist, but their status and their functions have been radically altered in many instances—and not in favour of parliamentary government in the British sense.

Generalisations in such matters are perilous, particularly since these young countries are still in a state of flux, but certain political developments may be said to have been common to many of them. The dominant political party has tended not only to monopolise power but also to identify itself with the Government, civil administration and the interests of the state as a whole. 'Oppositions' have either disappeared or have lost most of the effective political power they once may have had. And within the main political party one man has emerged as a strong and autocratic leader. Until February 1966, the former President Nkrumah of Ghana had been an outstanding example of this rapid and (to many) alarming movement away from the Westminster model. But Tanzania, where Julius Nyerere had earlier appealed to the West as a man who would tread the traditional paths of parliamentary government, is possibly an even more significant instance. Within a year of gaining independence, Nyerere had declared his country a one-party state. The Tanganyika African National Union not only held by 1963 a virtual monopoly of parliamentary representatives but was also identified, in practice, with the Government and the administration of the land.

The inevitable result of this absence of genuine party political conflict in Tanzania has been to depress the status and dilute the effectiveness of the National Assembly, where (to quote from the Report of the Presidential Commission on One-Party States*) 'with a few notable exceptions debates. . . . have tended to be lifeless and superficial'. Aware of these dangers, President Nyerere has tried to 'restore to the people the right to choose their own representatives within the context of a national political movement'†—in other words, the electorate may now choose between rival candidates of the same ruling party. Such constitutional developments prompt

* Quoted in *Documentation Series*, No. 3/65, Africa Research Limited, Exeter.

† *Ibid.*

the question: has effective parliamentary government, as we understand it, a future in Africa?

Time alone can provide a definitive answer to the great dilemma of African political development. But in the light of our own parliamentary history, knowledge of certain basic facts may help us to arrive at a more balanced and hopeful assessment of the long-term prospects for representative democracy in former British Africa than might otherwise have seemed possible. First, parliamentary government—despite its simple underlying principle—is in practice a sophisticated and ingenious instrument. The process by which in England executive authority was transferred from the king to ministers who, while remaining ministers of the Crown, nevertheless came to depend upon the majority support of an elected House of Commons, was neither quick, premeditated nor simple. Free institutions on the British model are among the most difficult institutions in the world to manage properly. It is certainly asking a great deal of a newly independent country to expect that it should accept without question, and with immediate success, the borrowed apparatus of a highly developed, centuries-old system.

Secondly, since parliamentary government is a legacy from a former colonial power, it is bound to appeal more strongly at first to the minority of those Africans who either participated in or understood the principles of British rule at the time, than it is to the masses of comparatively poorly educated Africans who look to their new leaders for political guidance. To many such people, moreover, the notion of 'constitutional' opposition to the main party—to TANU, for example, or to the United National Independence Party in Zambia—is almost a contradiction in terms, and seems to come perilously close to a betrayal of those who won them their independence. Such feelings, allied to the historical fact that in most of these countries the leading party antedated the arrival of parliamentary self-government and therefore tended to shape the latter to meet its own aspirations and priorities, are of extreme relevance to the present difficulties and (to outsiders) confusing political evolution. One must accept, too, that most African countries inherited from the British a highly centralised system of governing the country: the Governor and his advisers had been virtually all-powerful under the colonial régime, and it is undeniable that much of the authority once vested in the Governor has now been transferred—as a seemingly natural and inevitable process—to the dominant personality of the new African independent state.

Finally, and perhaps most important of all, it is vital to remember the great economic problems of Africa, the elementary position of educational and social welfare in many countries, the overriding need for cash and other material resources: small wonder, perhaps, that the tendency has been to unite behind one party and one leader. In this context the argument of a Draft Programme of the Ghana Convention People's Party 'for Work and Happiness' is significant, not least in its implied self-defence against criticism from Western democracies:

> Independent African States are faced with urgent and pressing problems of reconstruction. . . . This situation is almost analogous to a state of war and national emergency which is always met in the older established countries by the formation of coalition or national governments.

Under crcumstances such as these the vitality and primacy of parliamentary institutions are not easily and quickly established or maintained.

But these are still early days, and one of the greatest services which an old and established Western democracy can render its former colonies is to understand and openly sympathise with the very considerable problems which the latter are facing, whether those countries remain within the Commonwealth or not. A military government can be an unhappy innovation for a country like Nigeria which has known

democratic rule. But, as a leading article in the *Guardian**
has pointed out:

> . . . people in Nigeria and abroad who have admired that
> country's positive achievements in maintaining individual
> freedom will hope to see the Federation of Nigeria re-estab-
> lished in a more workable form.

Elsewhere, the very survival of parliamentary institutions
gives further grounds for hope. Such institutions have a certain vital force of their own, and this is also true of parliamentary habits amongst the people themselves. 'I have
sufficient power to be a dictator', said President Nyerere†—
but he added that the best safeguard against dictatorship in
newly independent Africa was the building-up and preservation of *a tradition of democracy*. Given reasonable social and
economic stability, many of these countries may well find that
parliamentary government offers the best long-term means of
maintaining national security and of ensuring social and
economic progress in the context of a *free* society where,
sooner or later, genuine conflicts of opinion are bound to arise.
Such conflicts may well exist beneath the surface already: but
the priority which emergent Africa feels it must accord to
the harsh facts of economic problems and of self-defence
tends for the present to stifle the free expression of such
differences in favour of authoritarianism.

A truly democratic and parliamentary approach to national
affairs would certainly spell delay and compromise; temporarily, therefore, the tendency is to thin the fruits of
parliamentary democracy rather than to cultivate them. Above
all, it is clear that Ghanaians, Kenyans, Nigerians, Zambians
and others want to discover their political and constitutional
future for themselves; intensely sensitive of their hard-won
independence, mindful perhaps of the colonial associations
of Western democratic systems, their goal is neither the

* January 18, 1966, p. 8.

† In a recorded television broadcast of January 20, 1966.

traditional African nor the black European, but the modern African. 'We intend', said Jomo Kenyatta, 'to make our own ideology, and we are free to take good things from all quarters ... I think the parliamentary system does suit Kenya, with, of course, modifications to suit the African way of thinking or way of life.'*

Meanwhile the 'precipitous climb of the people from tribalism to modern times overnight' is working itself out (the phrase is John Gunter's, writing of Nigeria in *Inside Africa*); but at the same time the survival of parliamentary institutions, and above all of the basic *idea* underlying them, is of prime importance. England's influence as the Mother of Parliaments, in this general sense, can still be considerable, and possibly decisive.

* *The Listener*. December 7, 1961.

Further Reading

K. C. Wheare: *Legislatures*, Oxford University Press, 1963.

Inter-Parliamentary Union: *Parliaments: a Comparative Study on the Structure and Functioning of Representative Institutions in 41 Countries*. Cassell for the I.P.U., 1962. (2nd edn., 1966.)

Sir Alan Burns, ed.: *Parliament as an Export*, G. Allen & Unwin, Ltd., 1966.

10
Perspective and Prospect

Dedicated as we all are to the modernisation of Britain, we cannot exempt the Parliamentary institution from these efforts. Modernisation, like charity, begins at home. Rt. Hon. Harold Wilson, in the House of Commons, April 2, 1966.

THIS SHORT and simple survey of a great and complex subject has taken us from the realms of theory, through the pages of history, into the bustling practical realities of British political and parliamentary life. It may seem a far cry from the statement of the *idea* behind all Parliaments, with which we began, to the tough realities of the struggle for power and to the personal, sometimes humdrum details of William Ember's busy day. There is an obvious distinction, too, between that same idea of the compatibility of Authority and Freedom on the one hand, and the slow, largely unplanned historical development of the Parliament at Westminster on the other. And yet all these disparate elements are inextricably bound up together to form that way of life which is known as parliamentary democracy.

The history of Parliament, as we have noted, is a legacy of intent as well as a legacy of practice: sobriety, caution, pragmatism are national characteristics which have not failed to mould and strengthen the greatest of our institutions. But love of liberty, a respect for the rights of minority as well as majority opinions, and a sense of the need for 'fair play' are ideological qualities, or aspirations, which are no less a part of the British Parliament.

There is to-day a good deal of criticism of Parliament and much debate, often serious and well informed, as to whether it is fulfilling its proper role in the constitution. But apart from anarchist, fascist and a few other small extremist groups, it is generally accepted that—whatever changes may be needed, and however urgently—Parliament is still a viable working principle. The severest critics assume and look forward to the continuity of the British Parliament, both as an established system of government for this country and as a much-needed example of practical representative democracy for others. 'Democracy', 'free speech', 'politics', 'elections'—the words are often used loosely, without a proper understanding of their constitutional significance. But few people to-day would willingly see them taken out of the vocabulary and practical context of British public life.

All power corrupts, and absolute power corrupts absolutely: the popularity of Lord Acton's words reflects the continuing conviction of the people themselves, who would not willingly surrender liberties—hard-won by Parliament on their behalf—to the authoritarian state. The late Professor Harold Laski once said that if all the criticisms levelled at the House of Commons were added up, the resulting impression might well be that Parliament should be abolished. But he continued that the alternative appeared to be the concentration camp. Indeed, the soap-box orator who addresses his little group of amused bystanders at Hyde Park Corner on the supposed iniquities and anomalies of the British constitution does so without peril to himself because he is lucky enough to belong to a country with established and firm parliamentary traditions.

The unrest which exists, whether justified or not, stems rather from a fear that Parliament is no longer performing, or no longer equipped to perform, its proper and vital functions. It cannot be emphasised too strongly that this type of *malaise* is as old as Parliament itself. At all times, and since 1832 at frequent intervals, the question has been voiced whether the current arrangements and facilities at the legislature's disposal are adequate. It is misleading and futile to look back to bygone days when—so the legend goes—Parliament had effective supreme power and worked perfectly into the bargain.

143

Every age, every generation, has had to face fresh tasks and challenges, and we can be thankful that the bitter struggles over freedom of speech in Parliament, over the ultimate control of finance by the Commons and over women's suffrage, are now no more than significant memories.

But it is also true that the great national and world issues which form an impressive and sometimes sombre setting for the pursuit and practice of parliamentary government in the second half of the twentieth century are unparalleled to date in their range and complexity. The Welfare State at home, the rapid changes of world influence under the impact of new social and political forces, and the giant strides of scientific and technological advance both in Britain and elsewhere are but the most obvious of contemporary challenges. Parliament's past strength and effectiveness have derived very largely from its ability to adapt its methods and its role within the constitution to meet the demands of changing circumstances: and the next chapter in the history of Parliament, when it is written, will be concerned to show how well, and in which directions, the British legislature has developed in response to the difficult challenge of the late nineteen-sixties.

This is neither the time nor the place to embark in detail upon the complex, controversial topic of parliamentary reform. It has been debated in the House of Commons itself on a number of occasions in recent years, and it has been considered in detail by the Hansard Society,* the Study of Parliament Group,† and a number of distinguished individual writers. But a few general observations of fact, as opposed to opinion, may help the reader—especially if he wishes to pursue the subject further—to view the question of reform in

* *Parliamentary Reform 1933–1960*, Cassell for the Hansard Society for Parliamentary Government, 1961.

† A private group of university teachers and officers of both Houses of Parliament, which has been meeting since the summer of 1964 under the chairmanship of Sir Edward Fellowes (a former Clerk of the House of Commons) 'to further serious study of the working of Parliament'.

perspective and to assess for himself the prospects for the future.

The whole purpose of contemporary pressures for reform is to ensure, not that Westminster breaks with its past, but that it continues to evolve by adapting itself and its business methods to changing circumstances and priorities. Frequently during its history Parliament has been compared to a living organic being. If the law of living matter is 'change or decay', then it becomes clear that genuine reformers are concerned for the survival and persisting vitality of Parliament—which will only be moribund when no one worries about it.

Secondly, it is important that all proposals for change should be based on a realistic, comprehensive view of Parliament as a practical and integrated working system. Any suggested reform—for instance, the setting up of specialist committees of Members to scrutinise the actions of the Government in various fields of public administration—is bound to have repercussions in other areas of parliamentary activity. Similarly, if it is felt that Members spend too much time on legislation, on the detailed examination of Bills, then proposals to streamline the passage of legislation through Parliament should also make compensating provisions for keeping Members better informed, better equipped to study and criticise the policies of the Government. Neither should the Second Chamber be forgotten—Lords and Commons together compose the legislature, and more than one writer has hinted at the desirability of having a *Joint* Select Committee, made up of peers and Members of the Commons, to consider various aspects of reform. It is dangerous to wish to make Parliament, like the proverbial curate's egg, good in parts.

The key to the success and stability of the British political system of government is its combination of strong central administration with effective constitutional opposition, and proposals for reform are only fundamentally sound and constructive if they take this overriding factor into account. No one doubts the power and resources of the Government—of the Prime Minister, his ministerial colleagues and of the vast machinery of administration which may be summed up by the word 'Whitehall'. Very few people, moreover, question the need for such strength. But the fear underlying most proposals for reform is that the corresponding need for effective parliamentary criticism and control of the Government is not being met. It is felt by many that a strong Whitehall must be balanced by a strong Westminster, and that the importance of vigilant, informed and *influential* parliamentary scrutiny of the Executive is all the greater because the Government is in Parliament and politically answerable to it.

As the machinery of central government is expanded and reinforced so it may become necessary to strengthen the resources and efficacy of the House of Commons—for it is there that the principal confrontation between Government and Opposition takes place. Those who suggest that the means of ensuring proper constitutional criticism and control of the Government should be reviewed and, if required, improved do not disparage in any way the accepted duty of the latter to govern. Put very simply the balance between the two must be correct—conforming, in fact, to what President de Gaulle described as 'the rules of the [parliamentary] game'.* Proposals for reform are therefore advanced in the interests both of good government and of effective, democratic surveillance by Parliament on behalf of the people.

A final generalisation on the topic of suggestion for change and reform is that they should be devised to support and strengthen the status and the working efficiency of Members themselves. The point is perhaps elementary, but it is well worth making. It is no use talking about the 700-year-old *institution* without realising that, at any given time, its character and its efficiency are shaped and determined *by the individual men and women sitting in Parliament*. Given the

* In his Address to both Houses of Parliament in Westminster Hall on April 7, 1960.

basis of free and fair elections, the position of Members of
Parliament as representatives of the people is incontestable;
and the interests of democratic government prosper or suffer
according to the manner in which each individual MP—on
whichever side of the House he finds himself—is able or is
allowed to perform his vital tasks. With the vastly increased
volume and technical complexity of public business, moreover, the presence of many full-time Members in Parliament
is rapidly becoming an accepted feature of the House of
Commons. As Mr David Steel (Liberal MP for Roxburgh,
Selkirk and Peebles) put it:

> We must be Members of Parliament first and any other
> interests we may have should come second. Only by adopting
> that attitude to the job can we serve our constituents and this
> House effectively.*

Changes in the procedure of the House of Commons, expanded and strengthened library facilities and secretarial
services, better working accommodation and amenities: all or
any of these developments, if decided upon, should be geared
to the specialised needs and responsibilities of the 630 men
and women who, after all, *are* Parliament during their period
of membership.

Both individually and collectively Members have always
been a cornerstone of the parliamentary system. To-day they
must function under very different (and probably much more
testing and trying) conditions from those which obtained
even 50 years ago. But neither the overwhelming range, technical complexity and pressure of public affairs, nor the strict
organisation of party politics, can stifle the importance of the
Member for Dorset East: even though such factors have undoubtedly changed his role, redirected at least some of his
energies and initiative into new channels of parliamentary
activity, and exposed him as an individual to those difficulties,
delays and personal frustrations inevitably associated with the
need for strong government and coherent, unified opposition.

* H. C. Debates, August 3, 1965, c. 1455.

He may not have 'power'—but he has influence. His place in the constitution, both as the representative of his constituents and as an equal Member of the 'House'—still a strong and meaningful term at Westminster—is assured, provided he is enabled and allowed to carry out the duties entrusted to him.

If the reader doubts this claim, he should recall that, since the House of Commons can change its procedure at any time, a majority of Members in Parliament could make it impossible for the Opposition to perform its vital task by condemning criticism of Government policy as improper and disorderly. Such happenings are not unknown abroad. 'We can never really be in danger till the forms of Parliament are made use of to destroy the substance of our civil and political liberties': the words of the anonymous eighteenth-century writer 'Junius' are equally apposite to-day. That a catastrophe of this magnitude appears unthinkable testifies to the integrity and ability of the average British MP. Voters will do well to remember that they are electing a *Parliament* as well as a Government.

This process of arguing from the particular (or individual) to the general (or institution) is also true, of course, of the citizen's whole attitude to Parliament and to politics. The successful canvassing of electoral support depends very much on the candidate's ability to appeal personally to the professional or to the working man, to the housewife, to the pensioner and so on. But if Parliament must continue to 'put itself across' to the people, it is equally imperative that the latter should accept the responsibilities, as well as the privileges, of a democratic régime. The late Jawaharlal Nehru wrote in his *Autobiography* that democracy, to be successful, must have a background of informed public opinion and a sense of responsibility. There are innumerable ways in which these responsibilities can be fulfilled—voting intelligently at elections, following the course of events at Westminster either through published reports and broadcasts or by attending occasional debates, making a sympathetic and proper use of one's own Member are but a few obvious examples. The simple point to be made here is that the people themselves, as well as Members, can be guilty of a dereliction of their parliamentary duties.

Parliament is Parliament. It is an institution which has both helped to shape, and been moulded by, seven centuries of history. Its underlying principle is that Authority and Freedom can and should be used in each other's service. It is not *the* Government, but it is an integral and (in law) supremely powerful part of the process of democratic rule. Parliament is the agreed constitutional forum for the attempted working out, in the interest of society, of those party and other political activities which result from the right of free people to differ among themselves. It substitutes discussion for physical force, and its ultimate aim is neither anarchy nor dictatorship, but government by reasoned and open majority decision. The British House of Commons is also, at any one time, the aggregate of 630 Members of Parliament upon whose shoulders rest the continued status and influence of Parliament as an institution. Parliament is, again, a way of life. Not only is it inseparable from national history, past and present, but its indirect influence is discernible in a great many traditions, habits, prejudices, virtues and vices of society at large. It reflects, but also stimulates and educates, public opinion.

If the British Parliament carried out to perfection, amidst constantly changing circumstances, the full sum of its duties it would indeed be no fit place for mortal men. It is imperfect, like all other things great and small which result from, and exist within, the human condition. It can and no doubt will be improved. It is not the only viable form of democratic government, neither is it entirely suited in every detail to the different requirements and priorities of all overseas countries. But Parliament's virtues substantially outweigh its weaknesses, and its value as a working example to a world which is witnessing the downfall or visible decline of free institutions in so many lands is beyond doubt.

Further Reading

A. Hill and A. Whichelow: *What's Wrong with Parliament?*, Penguin Special, 1964.

Bernard Crick: *The Reform of Parliament: the Crisis of British Government in the 1960's*, Weidenfeld and Nicolson, 1964.

Political Quarterly: *Special Number on Parliament*, July–September 1965, (Articles by Sir Edward Fellowes, Bernard Crick, Geoffrey Marshall, G. R. Strauss, MP, R. Hornby, MP, Michael Ryle and others. Bibliography by Anthony Barker.)

Index

Index

153

154

156